F. Mike Brennan
Easter 1974

creative fishing

creative fishing

CHARLES J. FARMER

Stackpole Books

CREATIVE FISHING

Copyright © 1973 by
The Stackpole Company

Published by
STACKPOLE BOOKS
Cameron and Kelker Streets
Harrisburg, Pa. 17105

Printed in the U.S.A.

Library of Congress Cataloging in Publication Data

Farmer, Charles J
    Creative fishing.

    Bibliography: p.
    1. Fish ponds. 2. Fishing. I. Title.
SH159.F32   639'.311   73-9836
ISBN 0-8117-0458-0

To Kathy—
the best wife and hardest working partner a guy could ever hope
for. Without her I would still be working on Chapter One.

Contents

Acknowledgments   10

Introduction   11

1   A Fish Pond—What Is It?   13
    A Christening   15
    Fish Ponds and Definitions   17
    Pond Sizes and Depths   18
    Pond Categories Based on Water Temperature   20
    Water Quality   21
    The Pond as an Ecological Showcase   22

2   Why Want A Fish Pond?   23
    An Opening Day at Bennett Springs   25
    Today's Fishing—Pressure and the Competitive Trend   26
    The Many Advantages of a Private Pond   29

3   How to Build the Fish Pond   32
    Where to Begin   32
    Looking for the Pond Site   33
    What to Look For   What to Avoid

The Fishing Pond and Its Features   38
   Dam   Inlet   Outlets   Other Features
Birth of the Fishing Pond   44
The Expense   46

4   **Where to Build the Pond**   48
What Is Quality Fishing?   49
Recent Trends in Pond Construction   54

5   **Who Will Help Build the Pond?**   56
Soil Conservation Service   57
Bureau of Sport Fisheries and Wildlife   58
State Game and Fish Department   61
Agricultural Conservation Program   63
Others Who Might Help   63

6   **About Pond Costs**   66
Land Purchase   66
Construction   70
Pond Management   73
A Typical Account   74

7   **Fish Stocking**   77
Stocking Cold Water Species   78
Stocking Warm Water Species   84

8   **Pond Fishing**   91
When to Start   94
The Pond's Carrying Capacity   94
Catching Trout   96
   Tackle   Rainbow Trout   Brook Trout
   Ice Fishing
Catching Bass   100
   Tackle
Catching Bluegill   103
   Tackle   Ice Fishing
Catching Channel Catfish   105
Facts From a Survey   106

9   **Making Money**   107
Fee Fishing   108
Raising Bait Minnows   111
Fish Farming   114

10   **Fish Pond Ecology and Conservation**   117
Ecology—Definition   117
Conservation—Definition   118
Ecology and the Pond   119
Conservation, Ecology and the Pond   120

11   **Pond Management**   127
Fertilization   128
Fertile Bloom Versus Turbidity

Fertilizing the Pond   133
  What to Use   How to Do It   Weeds—Good for
  Nothing   Excess Acidity Harmful
  Fish Need Air
Pond Management for Fish Production   141
  Feeding Fish   Managing Fish   Managing People

12 **Trouble Shooting**   **146**
  Disease and Parasites   146
  Trouble Shooting Fish Problems   148
  Trouble Shooting Pond Problems   151
  Pond Area Trouble Shooting   153

13 **What Pond Owners Say**   **155**
  Utah   156
  California   157
  Oregon   158
  Michigan   159
  Arkansas   159
  Vermont   160
  People Problems   164
  On the Good Side   165

14 **Pertinent Laws and Liability**   **167**
  Water Laws   168
  Fishing Laws   172
  Laws Regarding the Pond Itself   175

15 **Fun With Fish**   **179**
  Observing and Learning About Fish   180
    Trout   Bluegill   Bass
  Ecology   186
  Underwater Observation   188
    Snorkeling   Scuba Diving
    Underwater Photography

Bibliography   **190**

Acknowledgments

I wish to thank first the most important contributor to this book—my wife. Her research was untiring and diligent. My sincerest thanks and appreciation is extended also to personnel of the Soil Conservation Service—leaders in the field of fish pond planning and management. Their cooperation in providing current, accurate data and photographs was superb.

Thanks also to the Bureau of Sport Fisheries and Wildlife and State Game and Fish Departments—agencies that supply potential lunkers to fish pond owners.

And finally thanks to the many fish pond owners who took time out from fishing to answer my questions. I wish them, and all who helped, the best fishing ever.

Charles J. Farmer

Introduction

Creative Fishing is a unique book. For it is the first and only easy to read book for outdoorsmen who crave their own chunk of nature and the bonus of better fishing. The difference between this fishing book and others that have been published is that its pages describe to anglers everywhere how they can create their own, private, personal world of fishing.

That's right. Anglers caught in the "fishing pressure squeeze" can breathe freely again. Why? There are fish ponds just waiting to be built and fighting fish ripe for stocking. The fifteen chapters of this book describe each and every step to pond-creation—from land purchase, to dam building and what species of fish to stock.

Far from a technical volume, the book is prepared in an entertaining, light style with many first-hand examples of fish ponding. Fishing stories are plentiful. And tales of red-hot pond fishing highlight this practical, step-by-step method of creative fishing.

1 | *A Fish Pond—*
What Is It?

NESTLED IN A SETTING OF VIBRANT SPRING GRASS AND GUARDED BY a stately grove of budding walnut trees, the pond shimmered in the early light. It glittered, diamond-like, a jewel in the summer landscape. I remembered another June some years back. But now it had been nearly two years since the pond was first stocked with largemouth bass and bluegills. Like a peach tree heavily laden with ripe fruit, the pond was ready for picking. For months I had watched big bass cruise the clear water. And more than once they thrashed the surface with head-shaking fury to inhale grasshoppers blown to the surface by gusty Kansas winds. Then I'd catch grasshoppers and find an occasional worm to toss to the monsters. Just to see them methodically gulp these offerings as they sank below the surface. At times the temptation to fish was almost too great to stand, especially when watching those lunker bass swim unmolested, dining at their leisure,

13

while the largemouths at Johnson County Lake were giving me fits with their uncooperative attitudes. But we had made a promise in our family. The new pond needed growing time and we dared not wet a line in the fertile water until June.

For several years we had discussed the virtues of building our own pond. Fishing was our favorite pastime and we had the land. The location and soil was right for a pond and we longed for a good fishing place to call our own. The public lakes seemed to get more pressure each year and fish catching there was far from consistent. So we did it. With the help of the Soil Conservation Service (SCS) and the U.S. Fish and Wildlife Service our dream pond became a reality. The toughest part of the venture was waiting—from the time the Fish and Wildlife Service stocked it until it was ready to be fished. Not that we didn't have anything to do with the pond during that time. There was, in fact, plenty to do. We frequently checked the fertility of the water and seined the pond on several occasions to check fish growth. Then we planted the watershed with native grass, shrubs and trees to prevent erosion. The area, once a barren looking gully with a small stream trickle running through it, became a place of beauty.

The pond area blossomed the second year. The grass did well and the trees and shrubs, although yet mere infants in their development, budded for the first time. It was during that second year that my sister discovered raccoon tracks down by the water's edge. A pair of mallards nested on the bank that spring. One morning, early in April, a whitetail fawn sipped water down by the spillway. That was the first deer anyone had ever seen in the area. Like a magnet the pond was drawing wildlife.

I set up a small natural blind near the spot where the stream runs into the pond and photographed several varieties of shorebirds that summer. Rail, snipe and avocets were frequent visitors to the water. And on one rare occasion, I even intercepted a coyote on his way to drink, but as he cautiously approached the pond, the click of my shutter spooked him away. There was more to the pond than catching fish cruising beneath its surface, but I longed for that first day of June—the day when I could see just how big those bass and bluegill really were.

A CHRISTENING

June came and with it a fitting day for christening our fish reserve. It had been an unruly, cool, damp Kansas spring but that day was pleasantly soothing. It seemed as though every butterfly had come to life. Meadowlarks signaled warmth from every fence post and I couldn't rig my two-piece spinning outfit fast enough.

I tied on a medium-sized yellow Flatfish, a good bass lure for these parts. I'd concentrate on bluegill another time. A light wind ruffled the pond making it impossible to see beneath the surface. But that did not dampen my enthusiasm.

The light balsa lure floated with the wind until it splashed to the water about 50 feet from the bank and shimmered to a stop. I let it float momentarily to gather slack line and then began the retrieve. Perhaps it was the sight of their first lure that spooked the fish, but my first cast produced nothing. Nor did the second cast. "What's going on here," I thought to myself. "I've waited two years for this chance and now the fish are not cooperating."

Several more casts failed to produce a strike and I was beginning to wonder if someone had slipped down to the pond before the formal "opening" and caught every fish.

I changed lures, snapping a weighted silver spinner to the line. Able to cast it twice as far as the Flatfish, I let it sink before starting its retrieve. As soon as I picked up the slack line, a fish slammed the spinner hard. For a second my willowy rod doubled. Then it bounded back straight. "Lost him," I said to myself. But then the fish hit again. And this time I set the hook with determination.

It was easy to realize the fish had never been hooked before. He fought like an unbroken horse, but electing to buck for bottom rather than display any aerial tactics. Within a few minutes I had the fish coming. Anxious to see him I horsed him along rather than play games. When the fighter had been finally slid onto the bank I stood amazed over the biggest bluegill I had ever seen. The scale in my tacklebox put the slab-sided scrapper close to one pound. As wide as my outstretched hand from pinky to thumb, I could not help but gawk over the brute size of that bluegill before slipping him into the live net and making another cast.

As the spinner fluttered to the bottom monofilament line suddenly raced from the spool. I cranked the handle to flip the bail and reared back. The tight line began angling towards the surface and a fish exploded on top with open-mouthed fury. For a moment I saw the shining blade of my spinner dangling in the bass's mouth as it reached the crest of its jump. The fish submerged briefly only to lunge for the sky again. Although not leaping as high as before, he landed with side-slapping authority. I brought him in carefully and slipped a landing net beneath him while he lay thrashing at my feet. The scales read a bit over three pounds. The fish was thick and powerfully built—a handsome, healthy specimen of fertile pond water. Fat and well nourished, he was typical of the 13 other bass and eight bluegill I took from the pond that morning. Although not the biggest bass, I took the pond's first largemouth to the taxidermist. The fish was the result of a dream—a desire for private, personal fishing.

Even today the pond that had lulled me into those pleasant past June memories is nearly as productive as it was eight years ago when I caught the first bass from it. Some things, of course, have changed. The trees and shrubs are mature. The pond's waters, however, are still healthy and fertile. Countless bass and bluegill have come from its one and a half acres. My close friends have delighted in full stringers. And young children, craving the thrill of catching their first fish, have feasted on scrappy bluegill. The pond has afforded me and my family eight years of fishing enjoyment. And, if regular pond management practices are employed, we can expect many more years of fast fishing.

As I soaked up the natural beauty of the pond that spring day, I thought of other fishermen and those who love the outdoors. They could enjoy the same fishing. The world of the fishing pond can be shared within the covers of this book. Home-grown, home-sweetened fishing just might be your ticket "back to the land." It might be the way to beat the pressure on today's public waters. It takes merely the right piece of land, assistance from the right government sources and a little bit of your time. The rest is up to nature. For the farmer, the rancher, the ecologist, the weekend fisherman, the everyday angler, the city dweller, the suburban resident and the nature lover, the fish pond offers splendid treasures. Designed with the fish catching man, woman or child in mind, the pond offers numerous bonuses. It is a complete world in miniature—a breath of fresh air away from city smog. It is a model of nature's balance. It is—yes—a place to challenge fish. And a place to loaf; a place to dream; a place to bask on the grassy bank; a place to retain youth—wave a fly rod or a cane pole, dunk a worm or cock a number 20 Ginger Quill. The fishing pond is a refuge, a retreat and a handy tonic for mind and body.

FISH PONDS AND DEFINITIONS

Fish ponds are fish ponds. They differ from farm ponds, irrigation ponds, livestock ponds and water control ponds although they may encompass some of their features. Yet fish ponds are in a class by themselves.

Definitions can be cold, straight-forward clusters of words describing things in the briefest, most accurate way. Some may wonder what a fish pond is. Is it a delicate, statue-adorned pool of water encased in concrete—in which goldfish swim and lovers throw pennies? No, at least not in the definition contemplated in this book. Is a fish pond a place where fish are raised commercially, where perhaps they are trained to jump on the hooks of those willing to pay for the honor of catching them? No, not according to this writer, anyway. Is the fish pond an aquarium of sorts where fish and related aquatic life are put on display—to be looked at and observed in a controlled and very sterile atmosphere? On the contrary. The fish pond is a truly wild place. It is natural and so saturated with the good, intricate things of nature that it can teach us many things. And by following a few basic guidelines one can learn to create a complete habitat.

The fish pond within these covers is simply a body of water capable of supporting fish life and containing all the ingredients necessary for a healthy fish population. Water that supports fish life in a natural environment is quite different from that in a concrete fish pool full of goldfish, however. It is also different from that of a pond where fish are caught as soon as they are stocked. "Support" is the key word. It is defined as meaning a suitable habitat for the type of fish raised.

There are two kinds of ponds. An *embankment* pond is made by building an embankment or dam across a stream or watercourse. These ponds are usually built where stream valleys are sufficiently depressed to permit storing six or more feet of water. An *excavated* pond is made by digging a pit or dugout in nearly level areas. Because their capacity is obtained almost entirely by digging, excavated ponds are used only where a small supply of water is needed. Most fish ponds, however, fall in the embankment category.

POND SIZES AND DEPTHS

Fish ponds have specifications. One of them is size. This separates them from the common pothole. From one-tenth to one-fourth acre of water surface has been agreed upon by most SCS experts as a minimum size. Ponds of one acre seem to be a good average. Ponds smaller than one acre can seldom support enough fishing pressure to make pond management worthwhile. They are also likely to dry up or provide unsuitable habitat during periods of below average rainfall.

Size is an important consideration in stocking. Some conservation agencies, who would normally stock fish for free or for a modest charge, ordinarily do not stock ponds of under one-half acre. But my own reasons for a minimum size are these; the idea of consistently casting from one bank across to the other with little effort would take some of the fun from fishing. I'd also feel somewhat ridiculous launching my canoe in a pond only slightly larger than the craft, itself. So there's a psychological aspect to it. Somehow, for me, the old saying "like catching fish in a barrel" would come to life in a pond of less than half an acre. Then, too, from the standpoint of economics, it would be better to forfeit the pond rather than skimp on surface acreage.

There is a maximum size, too, for private fish pond classification; this is considered to be five surface acres. According to Ray R. Vaughn, Acting Assistant Director, Bureau of Sport Fisheries and Wildlife in Washington, D.C., ponds smaller than one-fourth acre or larger than five acres will not be stocked unless specially recommended by Bureau or state biologists and approved by the regional director.

Large ponds cost more to build, take more time, effort and expense to manage. A good guideline to follow might be that a pond with one to three surface acres will provide plenty of fish for family, friends, and neighbors. When fishing clubs or groups of anglers are contributing funds and skills to build a pond, several ponds, from one to five acres each, would be better than one larger pond.

A family-size pond might be considered a body of water from one-tenth to one-fourth acre of water. But this pond should be used exclusively for fishing. An advantage of this smaller pond for the family would be that it is easier to manage and usually produces more pounds of fish per acre of water. However, most families like to share fishing, so a bigger pond should be considered.

Aside from the surface acreage requirement, minimum depth

(SCS)

Living close to the pond doubles its value. The small pond is easy to manage and usually produces more pounds of fish per acre of water.

requirements are important for fish ponds. Some can be as shallow as three to five feet deep, depending on geographic location and individual state requirements. Factors considered in setting minimum depth include freezing, precipitation, weed and temperature control. Surface acreage and the water depth also have an effect on water temperature. Temperature, in turn, has a direct effect on the species of fish and living organisms within the water.

These important standards vary according to state. In Maine the minimum size for a pond is one-quarter acre with a minimum depth of six feet and a maximum bottom temperature of 74 degrees Fahrenheit (F). These requirements mean that the water would be suitable for species most commonly stocked in that state, namely rainbow and brook trout. New Hampshire, on the other hand, requires that minimum pond size be one-tenth acre and that a minimum depth of eight feet must be present over one-third of the pond. Requirements for local areas are available through the SCS.

POND CATEGORIES
BASED ON WATER TEMPERATURE

Fish ponds are classified as cold water, cool water, and warm water in the total scheme of pond management. Although the classifications will be discussed in detail in later chapters, the significance of these categories is worthy here of note—the class in which a pond falls, for instance, determines the type of fish stocked. Cold water ponds for example, where the highest summer temperatures six inches beneath the surface of the water is 70 degrees F, is suitable for rainbow and brook trout. Warm water ponds, where the highest summer temperature six inches below the surface is in the 80's and 90's, qualify for such warm water species as largemouth bass, bluegill, redear sunfish, catfish and bait minnows.

Cool water ponds, in the minority and not usually recommended for fishing ponds, feature a high summer temperature between 70 and 80 degrees F, six inches below the surface. These ponds are considered a type of "limbo" by conservation agencies in game fish stocking programs. Cool waters are not warm enough for warm water species and not cold enough for cold water species. According to L. Dean Marriage, regional biologist for the SCS in Portland, Oregon, "Channel catfish probably come as close as any fish for desiring cool water." Scattered examples of cool water ponds can nevertheless be found in most states. New Mexico, Arizona and Louisiana seem to have the largest share of them.

WATER QUALITY

Another quality that separates fish ponds from holes filled with water is that fish ponds are fed by reliable sources of water. The source can be natural, such as springs or streams, or man-made, like wells, runoff ponds and irrigation reservoirs. Whatever the source, it should compensate for evaporation, seepage, or drought. It stands to reason that the water source should be of high quality—that is, free from pollution, heavy silt and noxious gases.

The fish pond should feature a quality of water capable of supporting fish species native to the area or fish that can be successfully introduced. The availability of stockable fish native to the area relates to this reasoning. Managing a warm water pond for bass and bluegill in Wyoming, for instance, would be impractical, just as trying to manage a cold water pond for rainbow trout in Kansas. Private and state hatcheries specialize in the propagation of fish of proven compatibility to local waters. On rare occasions hatcheries may have experimental fish on hand, but it would be impractical and expensive for the pond owner to experiment with unproven fish.

This is not to say that only native fish can be introduced into the fish pond. Rainbow trout have done well in some traditionally warm water areas. And bass have thrived in a few typically cold water oriented states. But most fish stocking experiments are done by state and federal conservation agencies and pond owners should stock only species that have proven best to manage in their areas.

(SCS)

A fish pond is a place of retreat—a tonic for body and spirit.

THE POND AS AN ECOLOGICAL SHOWCASE

Perhaps the most complete formal definition of a fish pond is that it is a place of natural beauty in which a fish population thrives and whose waters attract wildlife of many forms. One SCS biologist calls the fish pond an ecological showcase.

The private fish pond is not a new idea. The Bureau of Sport Fisheries and Wildlife recorded the first fish stocked in farm ponds on May 12, 1949. Since then the popularity of fish ponds has been evident by the number of new ponds constructed and stocked each year for the primary purpose of fishing. In South Carolina, from 600 to 800 new ponds are born each year. Vermont adds 100 new ponds annually. Florida creates about 700 ponds per annum and Colorado adds 400 new ponds for fishing.

In the United States, private pond owners add about 35,000 new ponds a year. And now there are 3,000,000 pond acres across the United States. There is nothing new about the idea of creating ponds for fishing, but with fishing pressure increasing every year and good fishing spots at a premium, many anglers are creating better personalized fishing. At the same time they are adding beauty in nature. Man has taken from nature in the past and paid back little. Now—a delightful switch—the fish pond provides a two-way bond between man and nature. And man is rewarded by more creelfuls of fighting game fish.

2 | *Why Want a Fish Pond?*

SEVERAL INCIDENTS ARE FRESH IN MIND AS REASONS WHY WE FINALLY built a fish pond. But it was the trout opener at Bennett Springs State Park in Missouri some years back that probably was the clincher. I was working at the time for a chain of suburban newspapers in Kansas City. The work included a weekly outdoor column highlighting fishing, hunting and camping events in the Kansas-Missouri area.

The March 1 trout spectacle ordinarily meant interesting copy. Aside from a generous portion of rainbow trout ending up in creels, the human interest angle always provided good material. The weatherman, too, did his best to make the openers something exciting. If not a flake of snow fell in February, snow it would on March 1st. If the weather had been unseasonably warm and springlike in February, the wraths of winter would fall on that first March day. And so it was that hundreds of anglers would converge upon the Springs, spurred by visions of trophy trout like those conjured up in front of fireplaces during the rude winter months.

It was for that same opener several years back that my Dad agreed to accompany me to the Springs and capture the event on paper and film. Being somewhat of a fair weather fisherman, Dad was not overwhelmed at the thought of driving some 150 miles Friday night in order just to hear the siren that signaled the start of fishing Saturday morning. But he did it anyway. Maybe because I told him the fishing should still be good after we took a few pictures and interviewed some anglers. "Won't take long to get our limits opening day," I guaranteed him.

What I didn't tell him was that our chances were good to excellent for sleeping in the car that night. Accommodations are usually booked solid well in advance of the trout opener. The campgrounds would be wall-to-wall in canvas and it would likely be necessary to sleep a few hours in the car.

We arrived at Bennett Springs at 10 p.m. to find everything quite normal for Saturday's start. Accommodations were jammed tight. Super strings of tents, campers and lean-tos rivaled those seen at any major sporting goods show. Surprisingly though, the campground was quiet—all except for the grumbling of our car's engine as we maneuvered in and out, from one camping area to another. At 11:30, after four cups of thermos coffee, we finally parked on a bare patch of asphalt about a quarter mile from the stream. We were virtually surrounded on all sides by truck campers (their zone of the campground). "Let's stretch our legs a bit before hitting the sack," Dad suggested.

I had just about squeezed out the driver's side of the car when the door slipped from my grip. Although it swung only a foot or so, the sound it made when it struck the aluminum side of the camper next door was enough to make us both shudder. Almost simultaneously, a light flicked on inside the camper. A curtain parted and a face appeared in the window. I motioned a gesture of sincere apology, the face disappeared and the curtains closed as quickly as they had parted.

In the meantime Dad had gotten stuck while attempting to slip out of the car at his side. Finally, I managed to pry him back in. He sat for a minute exhausted, then we exited through the driver's door and headed for the store.

What a scene! Had I not known better I could have sworn that General Washington and his men were camped along Bennett Springs. Smoke curled from glowing embers. An occasional guard stood watch outside the tents—puffing nervously on cigarettes. Dogs barked in the distance. Somewhere a baby cried. From another corner came the low murmur of voices urging the kids to go back to sleep. "No, doggone it, it's not time to get up yet." Street lights near the store cast a hazy moon glow over the encampment. Their beams revealed the flicker of leafy-like snowflakes drifting to the ground. Already a white carpet was forming. Soon General Washington would order his bugler to sound reveille.

A piece of apple pie would have tasted good, but the store was closed. Back to the car and the chill of March 1st until an hour before daylight. Then a real pleasure to get out, to stand upright again and stretch cramped bodies.

AN OPENING DAY AT BENNETT SPRINGS

At 5:40 a.m. the siren wailed. The signal launched a volley of spinners, wobblers, spoons and flies. For several wild moments it rained monofilament. From the bridge overhead, we photographed the action. Anglers formed circles and semi-circles around the pools. Elbow to elbow they stood—men, women and children. We watched one veteran of the stream who had taken position at 4:40 a.m. to guarantee his spot. Soon another angler stood by him and the chain reaction began. At 5:05 a.m. the company was in formation. Latecomers were reprimanded to pool-tail positions. All except one middle-aged gentleman— shrewd, he was. We watched him work.

At 5:35 a.m. he casually made his way to the stream edge. A panicked gait would have given him away. His short, ultralight fly rod was tucked neatly inside the back of his hip waders. This was obvious only to persons not standing in the stream. An unlit cigarette dangled from his mouth.

Midway in the big pool near the bridge was an elderly gentleman smoking a pipe and chatting gaily with a shapely blonde angler next to him. "Pardon me, sir, do you have a light?" asked the latecomer. The elderly gent, surprised at the intrusion, dug in his fly jacket and replied, "Uh, I think so." By now the countdown had started. Wrists were being flexed as a warmup measure. Anglers stared at their watches. Last-second checks on line and lures were made. Elbows and arms were extended a bit to insure casting room. It was like basketball players protecting the ball in the last few seconds of a championship game. And all the while the old gent dug for matches. With approximately 30 seconds to go, the man pulled out a used book and gave it to the latecomer. The intruder held his ground and unsuccessfully struck one match after another in an attempt to light the cigarette. Then the siren's scream cut into the edgy early morning dampness and all conversation ceased. First-cast fish were thrashing on the surface. Lines were tangled. "Hey, you casted over me!" "Sorry." "I had a good fish on, too." "Is that my fish or yours?" "Think it's mine." "But I'm using a brown wooly, too."

While the old gent was courteously trying to untangle the blonde lady's line, our man with the unlighted cigarette stepped gracefully into his spot and began casting as if he were the first on the stream. He did well at that spot, too. He left 20 minutes later with a string of five wiggling rainbows. The old gentleman missed the easy fish of the opening hour and for all his efforts ended up with only one seven-inch rainbow (and a grateful blonde).

The crowd in and along the stream tapered off around 11 a.m. The trout quit hitting and finally an arm's-length of freedom spanned between the anglers. The stream now looked comparatively deserted. Despite the hour, we managed to entice some fidgety trout to the hook with weighted nymps. But it was evident that fishing now would be far from productive. The water had been whipped to a froth. It was time to head back home and enjoy some peace and quiet of the city.

TODAY'S FISHING—PRESSURE
AND THE COMPETITIVE TREND

Although it is not fair to pick on opening day trout holes, there are more Bennett Springs these days than most fishermen care to talk about. Trout streams and bass lakes all over the country have undergone attendance booms. Few hot spots are kept secret. And, as the result of more leisure time and better equipment, angling has become extremely competitive. "You should have been here yesterday" has given way to . . . "If you don't get here first, you may not catch fish."

Some fishermen like competition. For example, those who compete in fishing tournaments. And there is a minority of anglers who catch fish when others can't. But I believe most of us enjoy fishing at our own pace. Competition to us comes in trying to outsmart fish.

About five years ago, I inherited a fishing partner from a good friend of mine who moved away from Wyoming. My friend's parting words went something like this. "Charlie fishes all the time. Guess you'll be going with him now." Well, Randy wasn't a bad guy. We tipped a beer or two together when Jim was still in town. He talked fishing a great deal of the time. That spring when the streams opened in the mountains, I invited Randy along. Things went pretty well that first trip. We caught some nice brook trout. I caught a few more fish than he. But this did not faze me much. It must have spurred Randy's competitive spirit though. We fished quite a bit together that summer and each trip became more competitive. Instead of planning an assault on a stream together, Randy would mysteriously disappear downstream or upstream with a secret bait or lure hidden under his shirt. I knew better than to follow him. This would violate the rule of the game. The fellow who caught the most fish "won." And Randy was beating me on a regular basis and really working at it.

Several months later at a party I found out why Randy took such great pleasure in outfishing me. With a few extra beers under his fishing vest (he sometimes wore it to parties), he boasted how he could outfish an outdoor writer . . . namely me. "Now here's a man who makes his living fishing," Randy would joust, "and I catch more fish. Some expert!" I smiled as though the jab had no effect, but deep down it did.

After that night, Randy and I parted streams. I'm sure he thought I could not stand the pressure. And I couldn't. That's not fishing to me.

This is one reason I created my own fishing. I do not enjoy

This young boy is cutting his fishing teeth in homemade fish pond.

fishing pressure. When I found myself fighting more people than fish, I turned to my own pond.

Do you really want your own pond? The answer is probably yes. Let's say you live in a big city or in the suburb of a metropolitan area. The closest public fishing is 60 miles away at a state or county lake. It may be a nice piece of water. And the area around the lake may be well maintained. But for fishing—just plain tough and discouraging. The bass are small. There's too many stunted bluegill—nobody keeps them. And then there's the water skiers. After 10 a.m. the lake is choppy and the skiers are everywhere. Your state game and fish agency tries to keep the lake stocked, but there's just too much multiple use.

Then there's the farm pond you and your buddies may have fished. You met the farmer last hunting season. Heck of a nice guy. You asked permission to fish for yourself and a few friends and he obliged. The fishing for two and three-pound bass was great. And like a courteous sportsman you filleted some of the catch each trip and gave them to the landowner. He appreciated your efforts and welcomed you back. Soon the word was out about the fishing spot. A friend mentioned it at work. The group at Brown's pond grew larger and the fishing slacked off. But it was still a good place to go and you knew how to fish it.

Then early one Saturday morning you arrived at Brown's pond only to find the gate locked and a "No Trespassing" sign tacked to the post. Bewildered, you checked with Brown, himself, and found that someone had torn down one of his fences and scattered trash around the pond. He said he was sorry but that he had no other alternative than to close the pond.

Times are tough on today's fishermen. If shrinking habitat does not get the angler, rude, discourteous "sportsmen" will. Perhaps this is why the idea of a fish pond means more to a group of anglers from the city than it does to anyone else. Good fishing is at a premium. And urban and suburban fishermen need a change of pace from the city's complexities. The once-a-year, two-week vacation just does not settle the nerves nor cure the fishing fever like it once did.

THE MANY ADVANTAGES
OF A PRIVATE POND

Private pond fishing offers the city angler another choice. More than one band of fishermen have put their minds, wallets and fishing rods together to create good fishing. Many farmers, ranchers or landowners are willing to sell land suitable for pond sites. Weekend scouting trips can uncover numerous locations on the fringe of the city that are ideal for pond construction. And more often the price of the land, when cost is divided among interested anglers, is within reach of the average-income fisherman.

With the help of the SCS and the Fish and Wildlife Service, a group of sportsmen can produce top fishing for themselves and their families. Their time and effort creates a spot they can call their own. The fishing can be as good as they want it to be. Cabins, shelters and picnic tables can be erected on the site and a fair system of usage can be determined. By buying land and building one or several ponds on it, sportsmen's groups are guaranteeing themselves good places to fish for years to come.

Individual fishermen, depending on their income, can also

purchase tracts of land suitable for pond construction. One stipulation that individual and group pond owners should make when signing a land purchase agreement is free and unobstructed access to the pond. Other conditions of such contracts dealing with pond construction rights on private land involve common sense, rules of courtesy and respect for property and livestock.

If you are a fisherman your reasons for wanting a pond are evident. Ponds produce more and bigger fish than stocked streams. Ponds are more fertile, contain more feed, and provide a less strenuous atmosphere for fish than streams. It is as simple as that. The fringe benefits of pond ownership will also become important to you. For example, the pond in itself is a vital natural resource, a precious commodity within its banks. Life giving water—your water to develop and cultivate for the best harvest.

When prescribed management practices are applied, the pond describes in living color first-hand examples of ecology and conservation. Other forms of recreation can be derived from the pond. Duck and goose hunting in the fall. Swimming in the summer. Boating. Wildlife photography. All share roles in the life of a fishing pond.

Such a pond may prevent flooding. If properly maintained it will combat the number one pollutant on earth today—silt and sediment. Farmers and ranchers may build ponds for irrigation and fire-prevention. Ponds will relieve pressure on public waters. They can help anyone develop a more complete understanding of fish and sport fishing and its relation to the balance of nature.

The sheer beauty of a well landscaped pond is a delight in itself. No wonder Theodore Pawlowski, state resource conservationist for Vermont's SCS, said that, "The beauty of land and water is of primary concern. People have delayed construction of homes until a pond was built in order to better capitalize on the inherent beauty of the setting." The reasons are many and varied for wanting a fish pond. Some of the reasons are simple, but quite justified in a world often deprived of simple displays of nature. A pond is a resting place for ducks. It may be a spot to observe furbearers or watch the workings

(SCS)

A fish pond can add to the beauty of a property and be a long term good investment.

of a beaver or muskrat. The pond attracts raccoons, rabbits, doves, pheasants and quail. For some, the pond is a place to search for turtles, frogs and snakes.

The fishing pond is a world. And maybe you are ready to create one.

3 | *How to Build the Fish Pond*

THE PLANNING AND CONSTRUCTION OF A FISHING POND MAY INITIALLY appear to be a complicated and time consuming project. Let me assure you now that it is neither. In fact, as an individual or as a member of a group of sportsmen, you will be amazed at the simplicity of a good fish pond and the progress that you and fellow anglers can make within a few short weeks. Planning and construction costs are within the means of average income sportsmen. A chapter is devoted to fish pond cost later—no hidden extras left out.

Building a fish pond is interesting, but more than that, it is fun. For me, planning and creating a complete fish habitat uncovered many mysteries about the fish world.

WHERE TO BEGIN

The first and foremost step is to contact the Soil Conservation Service. This agency is a branch of the United States Department of Agriculture. Its personnel are proficient in matters of soil conservation—like the title says. Within the agency are specialists who deal with fish pond planning and construction. Properly managed ponds and watershed areas are tremendous deterrents to erosion, sediment, and silting—chief enemies of soil conservation.

Your local SCS office is probably listed in the phone book under United States Government, Department of Agriculture, Soil Conservation Service. It is best to deal with the local representatives since these men and women are familiar with your area. There are 3000 local, regional and national offices in the United States. If a local office listing cannot be found in the telephone directory, contact a regional office by letter. There is a regional office that covers these geographical locations:

National Office, SCS, Washington, D.C. 20250
Northeast Region, SCS, 7600 West Chester Pike,
    Upper Darby, Pennsylvania 19082
South Region, SCS, Box 11222, Federal Center,
    Fort Worth, Texas 76110
Midwest Region, SCS, 134 South 12th Street, Room 503,
    Lincoln, Nebraska 68508
West Region, SCS, 209 Federal Building, 511 N.W. Broadway,
    Portland, Oregon 97209

LOOKING FOR THE POND SITE

Some pond builders have gone out on their own looking for a pond site. Unless they happened to be construction engineers or persons thoroughly versed on pond planning and construction, this is how they made their first mistake. The local SCS technician is by far the best qualified to help select a pond site.

In all probability you or a group of fishing friends will be looking for a tract of land close to home. The acreage will be large enough to support one pond under five acres or, in the case of a large group, several ponds, each under five acres. Possibly you would like an area large enough to accommodate a cabin or shelter. Pond sites make good recreation areas when equipped with cooking grills and picnic tables. In the planning stage, when looking for land, consider a piece of real estate large enough not only for fishing, but for picnicking and camping, too. It will make the pond and the surrounding area worth more to you.

Keep in mind that while hunting for the right piece of property, land closer to the cities and suburbs will usually cost more money. You may be paying as much as $100 to $1000 more per acre for land close to home than for out-of-the-way rural real estate. But unless you plan to move to the country or build on your acreage, it would be smart to pay more money for land near you. The pond and surrounding area will be used more. Convenient fishing is worth the extra cost. After considering the additional gas and time needed to get to a remote pond, the higher price for closer land may be justified.

Some persons may already have a house built on a good pond site. Maybe you live on the suburb fringe. Or if you are a rancher or farmer, the pond sites may just await development.

Finding suitable land could present a challenge to the urban dweller. A good plan would be to contact several real estate agents in the area. Tell them what you want to do with the land. Explain to them that the land you purchase should have a reliable source of water, preferably drained by springs or seepage. Tracts with streams running through them will also work. Well water is fine, too. Of course, land with natural and man-made water sources built-in may cost more money than unimproved land without water. Real estate personnel know what land is available and the price of such acreage. Much of your shopping can be done by mail and phone.

Whether you own land already or have located land to buy through personal scouting or real estate reports, I recommend making an appointment with the SCS technician in the area of the proposed site. A good pond site is of primary concern. Inform the SCS technician that you are considering constructing a fish pond on the land. Ask him to accompany you to the selected sites. Chances are he knows a great deal about the land potential before even seeing it. And provided the price is right for you or your group, purchase the land according to the technician's advice. He may already also be familiar with land for sale that would make suitable pond sites. Choosing the best possible location right at the beginning will lower the cost of construction, stocking and pond management in the long run.

Also the SCS will inform you of the water laws and water rights associated with a piece of land. For example, can a portion of the stream be legally channeled into a private pond? (See Chapter 14 dealing with water laws.)

What to Look For

Pond sites are chosen according to available water sources, as already mentioned. But other factors are taken into consideration by the SCS. Low or seep areas too wet for crops sometimes make good sites. A gully may have potential, especially if conservation measures are built into the fish pond plan. As a result, the area becomes more attractive, and erosion is checked as the fish pond is born. Abandoned strip mines may have good fishing potential, along with suitable sand and gravel pits. At times reclamation land is available at a reasonable price. Pond building is a conservation measure that helps heal wounds and scars in the land caused by indiscriminate mining of metals and minerals.

General criteria used in selection of pond sites fall into three categories: topography, soil type, and water supply—features with which the SCS technician is especially familiar. Ideal pond *topography*, for instance, means a natural low area or broad draw with a narrow neck at its lower end. This permits runoff and spring water to be impounded with a short dam across the neck. The most economical site is one that will impound the largest amount of water, of adequate depth, with the smallest dam.

Soil type plays an important role. Since the pond is an earthen structure for collecting and storing water, its dam, sides and bottom should be composed of soils that will provide a watertight basin. Soils that contain enough clay, when properly compacted, discourage seepage. However, areas that appear especially suited to hold water sometimes cause problems. Areas with rock outcroppings, limestone, shale ledges and sand or gravel may cause excessive seepage and pond failure. If this is the case, the SCS man may recommend sealing the dam and pond bottom with a layer of clay, salt or bentonite. An important feature of pond planning, soil studies should be made only by those expert in making detailed soil investigations.

Ordinary small springs or seeps are the most desirable *sources of pond water.* These usually provide cool, clean, unpolluted water with an adequate supply of oxygen.

If springs or seeps are not available, surface runoff can be used. However, it is especially hard to control the amount of water entering the pond by this method. Diversion terraces can be used to direct some of the water away from the pond if there is an excess. If there is too little water entering the pond via surface runoff, the drainage area may be increased by diverting water to the pond from an adjacent watershed.

The drainage of a permanent stream is not desirable. Streams that drain large watersheds (areas where the stream cuts through) are subject to flooding during periods of heavy rainfall. Impounding such streams usually calls for an elaborate and expensive system of dams and spillways. In addition, fish management in ponds constructed from dammed-up streams is

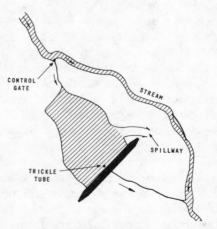

Typical pond plan where stream is water source.

difficult. Uncontrolled flows, siltation and the admittance of undesirable fish are problems. When a stream is used as the source of pond water, the needed quantity should be piped or channeled into the pond. The rest of the water is then diverted around the pond. Or the pond can be dug at one side of the stream and the water diverted into it.

When natural water sources, such as runoff, springs, ditches or seeps are not available, wells may serve the purpose. In some areas, wells serve as excellent sources of water for ponds because they come from a nutrient-rich stratum. On the other hand, some well and spring water is low in oxygen and may be charged with carbon dioxide or other harmful gases. Running such water over rocks or baffles reduces carbon dioxide and some of the other gases, and adds oxygen. The SCS will make water quality tests before pond plans are formulated.

The watershed is that land surrounding the source of water. When selecting a pond site, it is best to choose a watershed protected by forest cover. The result is clear, silt-free water running into the pond. On the other hand, watershed that receives hard agricultural use is poor. Croplands that are frequently plowed or tilled during times of rainfall mean silt, sediment, pesticides and agricultural fertilizers entering and polluting the water. Row crops induce rapid runoff and erosion and thus may damage ponds.

All agricultural land however does not make bad watershed for fish ponds. Grasslands hold soil and contain most runoff although not as effectively as forested areas. In choosing land for the total pond environment, look for good watershed. It will produce better fishing. You can control erosion and silting in the immediate pond area by planting grasses, trees and shrubs.

What to Avoid

There are other factors to consider when choosing a pond site. Avoid building the pond in an area drained by farms, feed lots, corrals, sewage lines and mine dumps. Avoid areas where pipelines and cables are buried. If uncertain about an area to be excavated, notify the utility company before starting construction. Otherwise, excavation equipment could disrupt utility service or cause injury. Chances are your SCS planner will have taken this matter into consideration.

Avoid building a pond under a powerline. Who would want a pond under a powerline? Nobody. But the number of ponds I have fished with powerlines dangling over them are too numerous to mention. Powerlines are dangerous and expensive to fishermen. Several of the ponds I fish regularly have powerlines overhead adorned with every type of lure, sinker, hook and line imaginable. One pond in particular has a powerline about 50 feet high, strategically positioned 40 feet or so in front of the dam and running the length of the embankment. To this day, I charge the owner of that pond with trying to collect enough lures to open up a tackle shop. The wire is ornamented like a Yule tree. Each new lure or coil of line added to the nest makes the trap deadlier. About 95 percent of the time, the baits cast glide harmlessly under the powerline. About five percent though are victimized by sudden gusts of winds. Some are trapped due to a premature reel-finger release. Never seems to fail that the trapped lure was the proven best fish catcher of the day.

Finally, in choosing a pond site, remember accessibility. Can you drive to the pond? Are there periods of the year when rain, snow or other obstacles make it impossible to get to the pond? Maybe the pond is within walking distance? Possibly you want it this way. Will the landowner let you travel his road to get to your pond? These things should be answered before construction is started.

When ponds and dams are built under the supervision of the SCS, safety factors are taken into consideration. Obvious violations of rules for safe pond location would be building a pond where failure of the dam could cause loss of life, injury to persons or livestock, damage to residences or industrial buildings—railroads, highways or interrupted use or service of public utilities.

THE FISHING POND AND ITS FEATURES

For a clearer understanding of the scope of fish pond worlds, the prospective owner should be familiar with construction procedures and how various features of the pond fit together.

The pond site, itself, is first cleared of all trees, brush and debris before construction starts. This leaves the bottom smooth for seining and weed control, which may be required later for proper fish management. It also prevents snags which could result in lost fishing tackle.

The topsoil is ordinarily removed from the dam site in order to secure the bond between the base of the dam and the pond bottom. After this step, the cutoff trench is dug, then refilled and packed with watertight soil.

When this is accomplished, the mechanical spillway or trickle tube is installed. The drainpipe, ordinarily part of the trickle tube mechanics, is installed and fitted with cutoff or anti-seep collars. These are placed along the drainpipe every 10 to 25 feet to prevent seepage. They are made from steel plates which are welded to the pipe to insure watertight connections.

Dam

The earth dam is then constructed. Soil material for fill is of proper texture, free of woody or other organic matter. Organic

(SCS)

Banks of dam are sloped on 3:1 ratio. This dam was built wide enough to be used as roadway.

matter in fill material will eventually rot and may later cause dam leakage. The fill is spread in layers about four to six inches thick. Then it is thoroughly compacted. Since this material will settle, the constructed height of the dam is increased by approximately 10 percent.

Earthen dams have extra freeboard height above normal water level to prevent waves and flood water from flowing over the dam and damaging it. Minimum elevation at the top of a settled dam is at least one foot above the water surface in the pond when the emergency spillway is flowing at designed depth.

Earthen dams are constructed with side slopes that prevent sloughing. That is, the slope permits water to drain off the dam. The accepted side slope used in construction is 3:1 on both the upstream and downstream sides of the dam.

The top width of the dam usually depends on the height of the dam itself. The minimum top width for a dam less than 10 feet high, for example, is eight feet. For a dam 20 to 25 feet high, the minimum top width would be about 12 feet. These widths prevent serious damage from burrowing animals, like muskrats, and nutria. It may also be desirable to make the top of the dam wider so that it can be used as a roadway.

Through the SCS, plans for earthen fish pond dams are usually reviewed and approved by registered professional engineers. Recommendations are then made for the best type of inlet and outlets to the fish pond to insure a practical, smooth-running, life-promoting habitat for fish and other forms of wildlife.

Inlet

As mentioned earlier, a pond supplied by runoff, springs or a stream may yield excessive flows of water into the pond. Therefore some ponds are equipped with controls to divert water not needed. If the water comes from a stream, an off-channel site should be selected for the pond, reducing most of the flow. If further flow reduction is needed, a control gate can be installed in the off channel. A grate placed at the inlet, big enough to be easily cleaned, will prevent passage of large rough fish.

Outlets

Outlets for the pond are handled by the trickle tube (mechanical spillway) in normal conditions. An emergency spillway and drainpipe serve as outlets under heavy rainfall or pond drainage.

The *trickle tube* is installed to establish the normal level of the pond. It also permits the regular overflow to escape without damaging the grass on the emergency flood spillway. Most trickle tubes are designed so that all water flowing through the tube is drawn near the bottom. This feature prevents the

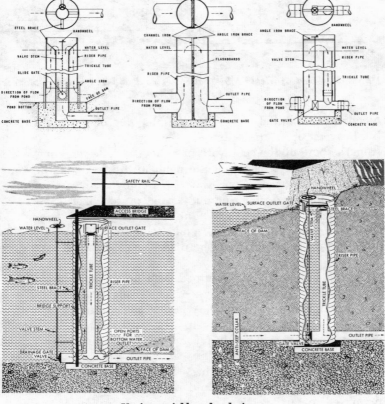

Various trickle tube designs.

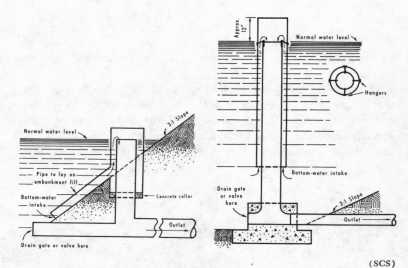

(SCS)

*Drop inlet—part of trickle tube that mixes cold and warm water and pre-
vents small fish losses.*

escape of fish and also prevents the plugging of the trickle tube
by beavers or floating debris. Since the tube takes outflow
from the bottom, the cool water is removed while retaining warm
water, which stays on top of the pond. In this way, warm water
fishing is improved. Cool water is removed or recirculated,
warming the pond in spring and saving on fertilizer.

The capacity of the trickle tube should be large enough to
return the water level in the pond to normal within 24 hours
after surface runoff ceases. The diameter of the pipe should be
at least four inches.

Your pond should be equipped with an *emergency spillway*.
The spillway carries off excess water during heavy rains. It is
large enough to handle the heaviest rains expected in the area.
For fish ponds, wide, shallow spillways are best. Less fish will
escape during periods of heavy rainfall with this spillway than
with a narrow, deep one.

A gently sloping soil is best for the emergency spillway.
And grass and sod cover should be established before water is
permitted to run over it. This will prevent erosion of the spill-

way area. Screening the spillway to prevent fish loss usually creates more problems than it prevents. It is better to lose some fish than to lose a dam because of a clogged spillway.

Many state regulations require a *drainpipe* in a fish pond. And on sound reasoning. It should be large enough to drain the pond in five to 10 days. As a fish management tool, it is well worth the installation.

The drainpipe is sealed with a breakable plug so the pond can be drained whenever necessary. For example, by unplugging the drainpipe the water level of the pond can be drawn down to control bluegill populations. In this way, many small bluegill will be trapped in shoreline vegetation and those remaining can be more easily caught as forage food by bass. Or when the dam needs repair or the pond needs cleaning, the drainpipe provides a valuable service.

Other Features

The construction period is the time to install features recommended by the SCS for successful pond management. It is easier to build them into the pond at this time to insure their working order than to add them later, having to drain the pond and lose fish.

(SCS)

Outlet with anti-seep collars and upright trickle tube.

For instance, many earthen dams feature a core and *cutoff trench*. This prevents excessive seepage of water through the soil along the base of the dam. The core extends the full length of the dam. The depth of its cutoff trench is determined during the time of construction.

Certain *conservation measures* are vital to fish ponds. For example, the top and sides of the dam should be limed, fertilized and seeded to grass in order to produce thick, tough sod. Good sod on the dam and spillway adds beauty and prevents erosion, which in turn keeps a fish pond free of deadly silt and sediment.

At construction time, many pond owners have trees and brush cleared from a strip 20 to 30 feet around the pond. This reduces the amount of leaves that fall into the pond. Leaves discolor the water and encourage growth of filamentous algae as well as using up the oxygen while decomposing. In fact, decaying leaves can cause oxygen depletion in the water. The cleared strip, when planted with a good stand of grass provides a favorable bank for fishing. Casting is easier. And when the grass is mowed, snake and insect numbers are kept down.

Trees and shrubs can be planted around the pond outside the 30-foot limit to enhance the beauty of the area. Fencing the pond will keep livestock out of the water, keeping it mud-free.

If you live in an especially cold climate where there is ice cover for a period of one month or more, check with your SCS representative about the need for a *pump or aerator* for the pond. Cutting holes in the ice is of questionable value since they do not admit much oxygen and quickly freeze over. You may want to figure in the price of a pump in the rough cost estimate. The unit is portable and does not have to be built into the pond. More will be discussed on hazards of freezing in Chapter 12.

BIRTH OF THE FISHING POND

With the steps already mentioned, the foundation to good fish management has been laid. When pre-filling, pre-stocking construction is completed and both you and the SCS technician

Steps in constructing a fish pond. First (upper left) a natural depression with available water source is dug and deepened for correct depth. Then (upper right) the pond is scooped and dredged so there are no shallow spots. This pond (not at full basin) (lower left) will fill and then be stocked with fish. Lower right: The pond is almost complete (sodding and planting the area is still needed). Posted sign aids in keeping uninvited guests away.

are confident that the water basin is adequate, pond filling takes place.

Filling is completed by several processes. The channel of a main stream can be opened to let in water. Spring and seepage water, which may have been diverted temporarily until construction was completed, is channeled back into the pond basin. Well water can be pumped, piped or diverted to the basin. And rain water does its share in the filling process.

Keep in mind that the depth of the pond, as advised by

your SCS will be determined by the climate and water supply in the area. Shallow water causes problems. Weeds grow in it and mosquitos breed there. A pond is easier to manage without shallow water. Either deepening or filling eliminates shallow edges. A combination of the two is best with the minimum depth of three feet being ideal.

THE EXPENSE

Obtaining a rough estimate of cost on the construction phase of the fishing pond is similar to obtaining a rough estimate on the cost of construction of a house. There are many variables. Your SCS representative will be of tremendous help in such estimates due to his experience. He can familiarize you with the cost sharing programs that may be available to you through state and federal agencies. Cost figures are rough but helpful in the planning stages.

Here are some services performed by construction companies. Types of equipment vary according to the availability of trained heavy equipment operators and the equipment itself. Pond owners pay for tractors, shovels or backhoes, and qualified personnel to operate them during pond construction.

Heavy equipment operators, following approved SCS plans, remove the top soil; grade the spillway area; mix the dam fill with clay; grade and tamp the sides of the impoundment to a 3:1 slope; tamp pond bottom for watertight seal; remove trees and shrubs from pond basin; remove trees and vegetation in a 30-foot swath back from pond shoreline; install trickle tube, drainpipe, concrete spillway (if recommended); install cut-off trench and core collars and perform other recommended construction services. A cost estimate of these jobs should be secured before construction begins.

In short, the brunt of the financial output of the fishing pond is encompassed by the initial land purchase and the cost of construction. Cost sharing guides and feasibility studies, available from SCS offices, will give an individual or sportsmen's group a good idea of the construction cost.

The construction company will build either an embankment

pond or an excavation pond. In only a few situations, where an extremely small water supply is needed, will a pond be excavated.

Machine operators following SCS-approved construction plans insure tight pond basins. Tractor, shovel or backhoe operators grade the pond bottom and build the embankment and banks to insure proper depth. Water-sealing clays and soils may be mixed into the embankment or lined on the bottom to insure minimum seepage. If possible plan actual construction of the pond during periods of good weather. Construction operators can perform necessary digging, grading and compacting phases in one continuous operation. Splitting construction chores costs more money and stalls the opening day of fishing.

Specific examples of cost are described in Chapter 5. Stocking, initially free of charge, and pond management help are inexpensive. Pond planning and SCS technical assistance are free. And prospective pond owners can receive free planning advice before they have even invested a cent. Rarely are such services rendered in any other form of construction or management planning. The fact remains that the SCS encourages construction of good fishing ponds and will help those who wish to build one in every way possible. The most important step in "How to Build a Fish Pond" is communication with the SCS in your area. There are no easy ways to plan or build good fishing. The simplest, most direct route to top notch private fishing is through the SCS.

(SCS)

At this stage of pond construction the trickle tube has been installed and grading and tamping operations are in progress.

4 | *Where to Build the Pond*

THE TECHNICALITIES OF WHERE TO BUILD A FISH POND HAVE ALREADY been discussed. Such points as described in Chapter 3 are important to the overall management of the fishing pond. Choosing a site with an available water source, watertight soil or clay and in a natural depression are vital considerations. Fortunately the prospective pond owner will have excellent advice from many sources. But the elements of planning and construction, although helpful in obtaining a complete mental picture of the pond, may not be as important to you as a fisherman as other aspects of where to build your fish pond.

Here's what I mean. In recent years the term "quality fishing" has gained popularity. It means simply this: factors that add to the worth of a sport fishing experience. Features of a particular stream or pond that make it something special—something unique, long to be remembered. Quality fishing falls into several categories and in choosing a pond site you may want to keep one or more of these ideas in mind.

WHAT IS QUALITY FISHING?

A quality fishing experience is a personal thing. It may not mean the same to all anglers. For example, there is one particular stream in Wyoming where I can feel totally relaxed. It is the North Fork of the Popo Agie (pronounced po-po-sha) near Lander. The stream is not well-known, except by Wyoming residents. Even then, it is not considered an especially good stretch of fishing water. The water I refer to flows through state and federal lands. It is fished rather hard by locals. But for some reason, everytime I fish and camp the area I feel as though I have been treated to a quality experience. It was not until a short time ago that I finally identified why the stream and the area did for me what fishing is supposed to do for all of us.

The public fishing and camping portion of the stream begins in a majestic chunk of real estate locally called Sinks Canyon. A blacktop road takes anglers into the canyon and into the Shoshone National Forest. The road is flanked to the north by sheer canyon walls. To the south, by the Popo Agie itself, willows and cottonwoods join the river on the south side of the stream and then the terrain ascends gently skyward. Alpine meadow joins with the carpets of green lodgepole pines. The topography continues skyward. The towering peaks of pine contrast sharply with the sheer, treeless granite cliffs on the other side of the stream. The diversification pleases the spirit.

The further you walk or drive up the canyon the less dramatically steep are the walls of the mountain and cliffs. Finally the land mellows near the top. That's where the blacktop road ends and a good dirt road begins. At this point I have reached my sanctuary. There is nothing primitive about it. Two well-groomed campgrounds border the river. There is a large parking area on the south side of the stream where backpackers leave their vehicles while they hike into the Popo Agie Primitive Area. This is as far as I have to go.

The swift, tumbling water of the lower canyon has softened into a flat, gently gurgling stream. The pools are big and deep. The water is so clear and pure at five-foot depths that the stream appears shallow.

At one of the campgrounds I usually put up a small canvas tent. About 80 feet from the stream, I can hear the gurgling song of water. Picnic tables, stone fireplaces with grates and clean restrooms are close by. Portable gas stove cooking by the light of a flickering lantern has a special meaning to me here. The campgrounds are nestled in groves of pines and although the road is but a few yards away, a camper feels snug—secure. In the warm seasons, birds and butterflies are numerous.

The fishing is not terrific, but it is interesting and challenging. A good catch would be four or five, 10-inch rainbow trout. They have been tempted before, of course. And fooling them makes an angler feel good.

Fresh trout fry golden brown in the skillet. Fried potatoes and onion accompany them and hot coffee is simmering on the stove.

Other fishermen and campers use the area. But the number seems small. People can catch bigger trout elsewhere. I'm happy that the quality of my fishing is not dependent on size. Seems like folks you meet on the Popo Agie feel the same way. Few rush to secret holes because there are none. Fishermen stop and talk to each other there. They even trade secrets. It takes good advice to catch spooky rainbows. And if Joe's No. 12 Hare's Ear Weighted Nymph is catching them better than Andy's No. 22 Blue Quill—all the better. Joe will probably give Andy the fly.

Quality comes in wading the stream. The pace—it's different. I take the time to study the pools like the "How to Catch Trout" books say. For once I realize nature around me. The moods of the fish don't change much in the Popo Agie. There will always be trout to catch. Carefully I admire the delicate workmanship of the No. 22 Rio Grande King dry that caught my first rainbow of the day.

Fishing the Popo Agie is a change of pace. That is what quality is all about. That area possesses elements which slow me down. The mountains, the water, the heady fish, the courteous anglers, the trees, the crackling campfires and the sounds of gentle rain on canvas roofs. This to me is quality.

Other factors produce an area that yields quality experiences. In the case of the Popo Agie retreat, it was more than just scenery and clear water that kindled my special feeling. It was knowing that I could reach the spot when I wanted to—whenever the need for a quality experience arose. Nor did I have to pack ten miles into a wilderness area. Regardless of season, access was possible. Permission to fish was not needed. The area was clean. The facilities of the campground were modern and sanitary. There I could taste the wilds, enjoy the challenging fishing and camping but remain close to the conveniences of town or city. There are few of us who would appreciate a completely wild, natural existence without the accustomed comforts. They are pleasant to come back to. Hot showers, running water and television are refreshing at times. Just as a trip into nature is a soothing change of pace.

So, perhaps it is just as important to look at the total area where your pond will be built. Will it serve as a retreat? Can you get away from noise, smog, smells, garbage dumps, hordes of people? Are there trees for shade and privacy? Can you keep the pond and its area private? Or will a steady stream of "friends" and poachers be infringing on your rights? The total look is important. If your pond, the fishing it produces and the area where it is built, does not serve as a nerve tonic—a place for you, your family and your thoughts—consider an area that does. Tall peaks, stands of pine or crystal clear water are not prerequisites. But quality to meet your needs and wishes is.

Just recently I had the pleasure of fishing and camping in Manitoba and Saskatchewan. Many of these areas my wife and I visited were remote, primitive looking and wonderful. In Manitoba, we especially enjoyed a place located in Duck Mountain Provincial Park called Singush Lake. The area featured typical north woods topography—rolling forested hills, muskegs, streams, willow marshes and clear lakes. Singush was a delight. We caught northern pike, musky and smallmouth bass. Loons echoed their lonely cries at night. Snowshoe hare abounded in the forest around the lake. And camp was set at a modern,

A good pond site is an area which is a natural basin. At this pond, fill has been used to stabilize a gully that once was ten feet deep.

clean campground. Despite all this, we found ourselves enjoying a quality environment with only two other campers. It was there that we found true north woods flavor. We had attained the quality goal of our trip.

From Singush we drove north hoping for more outdoor delights. There were magnificant lakes in the area. One tip at a tackle store in a town farther along spoiled its north woods image.

I make a habit of asking where I can find good fishing. Native anglers and sporting goods dealers are usually quite willing to share fishing tips. I was particularly optimistic when a tackle dealer at this place told me where lots of big northerns and walleye could be caught "within a few minutes of town." And he was right. The spot proved just a short drive from town.

I could not believe it when I got there. The town fishing hole resembled a sewer treatment pool. A portion of a river had been channeled and dammed, creating a stagnant pond. Some of the walleyes and northerns traveling the river followed the channel and were trapped in the pool by the dam.

My wife and I arrived at the pond shortly before noon—a time when most serious anglers are home cleaning their morning's catch. But the pond was lined with anglers. The area was devoid of trees. Two garbage cans at the pond's edge overflowed with everything from fish entrails to discarded cheese sandwiches.

"This is it?" my wife asked. "I'm sure I followed the right directions," I replied. But I still wasn't really sure. I decided to check with the nearest fisherman. The man closest to our vehicle was hauling in a 30-inch northern pike when I approached him. "Damn jacks," he mumbled to himself. "They ain't good for nothing. Too boney to eat."

"Pardon me, sir," I interrupted. "I stopped in town and asked where there was good fishing. Is this the spot?" "Sure is," the man replied. He knelt down and lifted a stringer of fat walleye pike for my inspection. "Caught all these right from this spot!" "Uh, can you eat the fish that come out of this pond?" I asked. "Oh, I eat 'em all the time," the man replied. "Some folks are afraid of the mercury. But I'm still alive, ain't I?" "You sure look that way to me," I answered. "Thank you, sir, and good fishing."

"This is the place, all right," I told Kathy. "But it doesn't smell too good out there. Those flies are everywhere. Let's sit in the car and watch awhile."

The fishing was hot. Everyone was catching big fish. Even as the noon-day sun increased the frenzy among the flies feasting on fish guts, one fish after another was hauled in. It was the best fishing we had seen in Canada, but we left after ten minutes. It was lunch time and this area was not conducive to good digestion.

The moral of the story? Quality. Fishing at this place was an extreme example—true. But fishing means more to me than catching fish trapped in dirty water. Most of us want more from our sport. That's why, when selecting a pond site, we look for an area with something special. With proper pond management we can cultivate good fishing. Careful pond site selection results in a good environment to match.

Not all pond sites are environmentally sound to start with but a good pond site may have potential for beauty. When creating good fishing, a pond owner has the option of also beautifying an area.

An eroded gully, for instance, is usually an eyesore. It certainly is not an area of beauty. But an eroded gully, provided its soil has good water-holding qualities, may have possibilities for a fish pond. Thus the pond owner can transform gullies into places of beauty. Trees, shrubs, grass and flowers planted around the pond complete the transformation. Rehabilitating a portion of land, regardless of the size, is a satisfying bonus to fishing.

RECENT TRENDS IN POND CONSTRUCTION

On a national scale, it is interesting to note just where fish ponds have taken hold. States that helped in researching this book, for instance, are among the top producers of fish ponds annually.

AVERAGE NUMBER OF FISH PONDS BUILT PER YEAR

Arkansas	2000
Colorado	400
Florida	700
Idaho	500
Iowa	900
Kansas	2000
Louisiana	1000
Maine	100
Maryland	150
Massachusettes	20
Michigan	1500
Mississippi	3000
Pennsylvania	500
South Carolina	700

Utah	35
Vermont	100

(Figures valid as of January, 1973.)

From these figures and other sources of information obtained from various states, a pattern of fish pond construction has developed. Perhaps your state fits into the pattern. In agricultural states, many farm ponds are constructed. However, in states of thin population, only a small percentage of the ponds are stocked with fish. For example, in South Dakota only .8 percent of the ponds built in 1971–72 were stocked; this amounts to 25 fish ponds out of a total of 3000 farm ponds built that year.

In Idaho 10 percent of the ponds are stocked. The reason for this is that the state is blessed with numerous streams and lakes that produce good fishing. Other mountain states with good natural fishing and relatively low population centers, fall into the same category. Kansas, on the other hand, not blessed with an abundance of natural fishing waters, has improved available fishing immensely by encouraging the construction of ponds.

As the population increases, more fish ponds are bound to appear and states that have not placed much emphasis on fish pond construction in the past will be devoting more attention to it. Even Alaska and Hawaii, states that reported having no ponds expressly created for fishing, may find a need someday to encourage pond building. But at present they do not feel the "fishing hole squeeze" that is so symptomatic of the lower 48 states.

Fish ponds have no geographical limit. And they can be built anywhere that good fishing and peaceful, natural retreats are desired.

5 | Who Will Help Build the Pond?

POSSIBLY NO OTHER PROJECT ONE COULD CONCEIVE IS AS MUCH subject to the availability of free, expert help and advice as fish pond construction. As a pond owner one of the most important steps in planning your pond is knowing what agencies can help.

The major share of help comes from three different agencies. The SCS is the major planner and should be contacted first. After the pond is filled and meets all SCS specifications the pond qualifies to receive stocking assistance from the Bureau of Sport Fisheries and Wildlife, a branch of the Fish and Wildlife Service under the Department of the Interior. The national address for the Bureau is simply: Bureau of Sport Fisheries and Wildlife, Washington, D.C., 20240. Like the SCS, it is divided up into regions—the names and addresses of these are listed at the end of this chapter. It is best to contact the appropriate regional director in regards to questions on pond stocking in your area.

The overall function of the Bureau of Sports Fisheries is to aid in conservation of the nation's migratory birds, certain mammals, and sport and commercial fishes. The Bureau promotes the acquisition and application of technical knowledge necessary for the perpetuation and enhancement of fish and wildlife resources. Since a pond owner performs a dual role as conservationist and fish perpetuator, he is entitled to help from the Bureau.

Another major contributor to the fish pond cause is the state fish and game department. Your local fisheries biologist, in particular, is a valuable source of information and advice. Perhaps no other individual in your area knows more about fish and their management than does the state fish biologist or culturist.

Aside from these major sources of help, the Agricultural Stabilization and Conservation Service, Washington, D.C., 20250, could be another important contact. According to specified guidelines, some fish pond owners qualify for financial assistance from this agency in planning and construction of farm ponds.

Private fish hatcheries in the area and other fish pond owners also lend assistance at various stages of pond development and management.

Specifically, here is what each agency can do for you.

SOIL CONSERVATION SERVICE

Services rendered from the SCS vary according to the state in which you live. Local SCS offices and technicians can help with various aspects of pond planning and construction.

In New Hampshire, for example, according to SCS biologist David N. Allan, many services are offered to the fish pond owner. These are site selection, survey and design, seedings and wildlife plantings, assistance in delivery, soil suitability studies, supervision of construction, providing recommendations as to the fish species and numbers to stock, pond management relating to weed control, feeding and stocking. They are rendered free of charge provided the pond owner puts the land under a conservation planning agreement. This agreement, according to South Dakota SCS biologist John B. Farley, is a plan with the local Conservation District that plays an important role in the larger more complete conservation effort. A pond owner can qualify for complete assistance, including staking for construction and construction checkout, provided he owns, leases or rents land and agrees to become a Conservation District cooperator. This means that in the planning and construction of the fish pond and in the management of that pond and the surrounding area, the owner agrees to apply all conservation measures needed as recommended by a local SCS technician.

In more simplified terms, when a fish pond owner follows the conservation techniques recommended by the SCS, he qualifies for complete assistance from that agency.

If an individual does not want to put his land under a conservation planning agreement or if the individual does not own, lease or rent the land where the fish pond will be located, the SCS is not obliged to render complete assistance. In this case a pond owner may receive only consultive assistance and appropriate SCS publications.

As seen in Mr. Farley's statement, it means that fish pond aid is granted only when the pond can be part of the total conservation effort. Most fish pond owners agree with this philosophy.

Since SCS services vary in each state, it is best to contact the local representative first. Some states offer free cost estimates, engineering assistance, coordination of fish orders with the Bureau of Sport Fisheries or private hatcheries, cost sharing guides and feasibility studies.

BUREAU OF SPORT FISHERIES AND WILDLIFE

The bureau will provide fish of approved size, species and number as available. It also establishes stocking and management policies and procedures for the fish pond program in cooperation with the SCS and state conservation agencies. Bureau technicians give technical advice and assistance.

In regards to stocking, the Bureau advises cooperating

agencies on species availability and maintains records of stocking applications filed by pond owners.

Certain stocking qualifications are defined by the Bureau. Farm ponds that qualify for federal stocking are small, artificially constructed impoundments which do not contain established fish populations. Trout ponds, for instance, must have at least one-quarter acre surface water, while the minimum size for warm water fish ponds is one-half acre. Ponds of over five acres are not qualified for federal stocking unless they are specifically recommended for it by the SCS. They must also be approved by the Bureau or state fisheries biologist.

Commercial fish ponds (fee fishing ponds or waters used to raise and harvest fish for food or bait sale) or ponds affiliated with commercial enterprises are not qualified for stocking under the provisions of the program. Warm water ponds that have been reclaimed by draining or chemical treatment will be considered as new qualified ponds.

The Bureau provides only fingerling fish. Trout are normally two to four inches long. Warm water species are one to two inches in length.

Rainbow or brook trout are available for cold water ponds and largemouth bass and bluegill are usually available for warm water fishing.

Fish pond owner stocking applications are filled whenever possible with the species of fish desired. But if a state conservation agency restricts the stocking of a particular species of fish in a certain area, the Bureau adheres to the state rules.

With this in mind, species other than the fish requested may also be provided if the pond owner agrees. In such cases the Bureau advises fish pond owners of the other kinds of fish they can deliver. This is a good reason for checking with the state fish biologist first before specific stocking plans begin.

Applications for stocking ponds under the Farm Pond Program should be endorsed by a representative from one of the following: State Game and Fish Agency, Cooperative Extension Service, SCS, or Bureau of Sport Fisheries and Wildlife. The official application form, available from an SCS technician or regional Bureau office, should then be sent to the appropriate regional office.

To qualify a pond for receiving trout, the delivering hatchery must receive approved applications by April 15. Applications for warm water species are required by June 1 in order to be included in the current year's distribution sequence (summer or fall stocking). Applications received after the dates mentioned are held over until the following distribution season.

At times there may be conditions preventing the Bureau from stocking private ponds. There are reasons why stocking requests sometimes may not be filled. One reason is that the federal hatchery in the area may not have a sufficient supply of fish on hand. Hatchery production is allocated on a priority basis, and federal and state waters open to public fishing are stocked first. Then the remaining fish can be stocked in private waters not open to public fishing, and not commercialized in any way.

Do you *have to open your pond to public fishing* if it is stocked by a federal agency?

State and federal stocking agreements differ. Most states do not require opening the pond to public fishing. Some require enough fishing be allowed to insure the adequate fish harvest needed for sound pond management. Some state hatcheries will stock fish but also require public access. The specifics of "people management" and how it affects pond operation will be discussed in more detail in Chapter 11—Pond Management. The SCS technician will, of course, inform you of the stocking requirements in your state.

The Bureau may not stock fish if the species of fish requested is not available or if the state conservation agency can supply the fish instead. Or, a pond owner may have failed to meet some SCS design, construction and pond management specification. But most of these stocking problems can be avoided by coordinating early efforts with the SCS.

In regards to the actual stocking of your pond, the Bureau explains the procedure to follow. Ordinarily one or more deliveries are required to fill stocking applications. The hatchery notifies the pond owner a few days before each delivery is made. If the pond is near the hatchery, the Bureau may request that the pond owner receive the fish there. Normally, though, delivery is made by a fisheries truck to some point in the area of the pond.

The stocking truck travels on a rigid schedule. Pond owners are requested to meet it at a designated time. Details on the containers used for transporting fish and the care of fish during delivery and planting are covered in Chapter 7—Fish Stocking. After the initial free stocking, fish delivery from private hatcheries may be possible directly to the pond site.

In most cases the Bureau supplies only an initial stocking. According to Mr. Ray Vaughn, acting assistant director of the Fish and Wildlife Service, Bureau of Sport Fisheries and Wildlife in Washington, D.C., trout and warm water ponds come under different stocking programs. The Bureau supplies only the initial stocking for new trout ponds, and all subsequent restocking is the responsibility of the pond owner who may, of course, acquire fingerling trout also from commercial sources. But pond owners are made acquainted with the policy prior to the initial stocking.

In regards to warm water ponds, Mr. Vaughn pointed out that normally his agency does not restock warm water ponds at intervals of less than once in five years. Reclaimed ponds, however, may be restocked without regard to this limitation. If channel catfish are used in the stocking program, the Bureau will make only an initial stocking.

STATE GAME AND FISH DEPARTMENT

It is apparent that the Bureau of Sport Fisheries and Wildlife respects the grass-roots-level of state conservation agencies. The state game and fish department can approve or disapprove stocking applications as they have final control over fish stocking. It stands to reason that a local fisheries biologist can give the best advice on fish stocking. This is his job. He is familiar with water quality, fish habitat, diseases and parasites of fish and the correct stocking procedures for a specific locale.

In areas of pond management, the fisheries expert usually has a complete modern lab at his disposal for aid in finding solutions to fish management problems. In matters of fish and

(SCS)

Bureau of Sport Fisheries and Wildlife helps with stocking programs.

weed control, he may advise appropriate toxics to use in solving some problems.

Chances are the SCS technician will rely heavily on the knowledge of the fisheries expert in the area. During the life of your pond, both of you will depend on reliable fish management techniques that produce the best of pond fishing.

Some state conservation agencies have fish available for stocking. As mentioned earlier, they may stipulate that a certain amount of public fishing be allowed if they are to help with planting.

If a pond owner does not wish to be a Conservation District Cooperator, it is the game and fish department that usually assists in filing applications for fish or directing the owner to the appropriate Bureau office.

AGRICULTURAL CONSERVATION PROGRAM (AS ADMINISTERED BY AGRICULTURAL STABILIZATION AND CONSERVATION SERVICE)

The SCS helps formulate this annual program under the guidance of the Agricultural Stabilization and Conservation Service. It is carried out at the national, state and county level. Basically the program is designed to share with land users the cost of applying certain soil and water conservation measures.

County committees accept applications for cost sharing and issue Agricultural Conservation Program (ACP) payments after conservation practices have been satisfactorily applied. Under the program, conservation projects that fall under the technical responsibility of the SCS are eligible for payments. Pond owners should discuss the possibilities of their qualification with the SCS.

(On January 30, 1973, C.A. Krall, Nevada Conservationist with the SCS, informed the author that, "The Agricultural Stabilization and Conservation Service Program was just recently closed out and no funds are available at the present time. Perhaps if you checked with the local office they could supply you with the most recent information concerning their programs." Obviously, payments under this program are dependent on funds available within the federal budget and budget management actions.)

OTHERS WHO MIGHT HELP

After the initial stocking the pond owner will depend on private or commercial fish hatcheries near him. Like most commercial enterprises, some hatcheries are better than others. Most hatchery managers are willing to help. Since they are in the fish rearing business as a livelihood, many are experts in their field. Do not hesitate to seek the advice of reputable hatchery operators. Your local fisheries biologist or SCS technician will recommend good private hatcheries to work with. Remember, ordering fish from unknown, unrecommended sources is gambling with the entire fish pond operation. Experimenting on your own with exotic species or fish not recommended by your local fisheries expert could damage your own pond's fishing and possibly adversely affect the public fishing waters of your state.

Other fish pond owners in your area may be sources of valuable advice and help. However, be aware that every pond habitat is different. What is good for your neighbor's pond or his fish may ruin your pond and kill its fish. In matters of fish pond management, consult fisheries experts.

Stocking another pond by transferring to it fish caught from a neighbor's pond is a serious mistake. Your pond is stocked by experts who know exactly how many fish the pond will support and what size is best for stocking. Introducing to it another pond's inhabitants might disrupt the entire fish population. And the chance of spreading fish disease and parasites is increased.

It is fine to compare notes with fellow pond owners. Some areas even have fish pond clubs to join. They are fun. But don't forget the experts. With their help your fish will grow fast. They will be healthy and the catching will remain good.

BUREAU OF SPORT FISHERIES AND WILDLIFE— REGIONAL OFFICES

Pacific Region, 730 N.E. Pacific Street, Portland, Oregon 97208

Alaska, California, Idaho, Hawaii, Montana, Nevada, Oregon, Washington.

Southwest Region, Federal Building, 500 Gold Avenue S.W., Albuquerque, New Mexico 87103

Arizona, Colorado, Kansas, New Mexico, Oklahoma, Texas Utah, Wyoming.

North Central, Federal Building, Fort Snelling, Twin Cities, Minnesota 55111

Indiana, Illinois, Iowa, Michigan, Minnesota, Missouri, Nebraska, North Dakota, Ohio, South Dakota, Wisconsin.

Southeast Region, 809 Peachtree, 7th Building, Atlanta, Georgia 30323

Alabama, Arkansas, Florida, Georgia, Kentucky, Louisiana, Mississippi, North Carolina, South Carolina, Tennessee, Virginia.

Northeast Region, U.S. Post Office and Courthouse Boston, Massachusetts 02109

Connecticut, Delaware, Maine, Massachusetts, New Hampshire, New Jersey, New York, Pennsylvania, Rhode Island, Vermont, West Virginia.

6 | *About Pond Costs*

IN CONSIDERING THE COST OF A FISH POND, REMEMBER THAT THE time and money invested is intended to produce a source of recreation that can last a lifetime. Not only can you as an individual or member of a sportsmen's group enjoy the pond, but, hopefully, your sons and daughters will also have a place to fish and absorb nature. In a time of shrinking natural habitat, even the smallest chunk of land and water is becoming a treasured possession. If wondering just how much such an investment would really be worth, just look at the costs of prime real estate.

LAND PURCHASE

Land in Jackson Hole, Wyoming, with good access and clear trout streams running nearby costs as much as $10,000 an acre. Granted, Jackson is an area of magnificent natural beauty with little private land left. But the fact remains that most areas offering good access and a variety of recreational benefits are at a premium. The cost of such land can only go up. Wise investors and shrewd real estate agents agree that good land is the wisest purchase a person can make these days. I don't disagree. The cost of a fish pond, however, is dependent on several things, the purchase of a suitable pond site and construction and material costs being dependent on geographic and seasonal criteria.

Many prospective pond owners already own land. Others purchase land for purposes of pond building. Cost per acre of undeveloped land with an adequate water supply source and satisfactory access varies according to area. But in no way do these costs compare to resort area land prices where the dollars per acre asked are hinged on the amenities of towering mountain peaks and clear trout streams.

Let us imagine though that an average cost of $600 per acre is a fair price for a pond site. This figure could, of course, be higher or lower. But it is somewhat of a norm these days for small amounts of undeveloped acreage. The price per acre would drop considerably if 100 or more acres were purchased. Or this price could rise if only one or two acres were being purchased. In other words, land sales ordinarily follow a quan-

(SCS)

Another instance where a fish pond has added to the value of house and land—a lasting investment for the future.

tity discount formula; the more acres purchased, the less the cost per acre.

Purchasing several hundred acres of land, except for agricultural reasons, may be impractical and financially impossible for most individual pond owners. A group of sportsmen from a city or neighboring suburb, however, may find that pooling their money and purchasing considerable acreage could be to their advantage.

For example, say that 10 fishing partners join together and purchase 100 acres of land; that includes suitable locations for one or several pond sites. If they pay $200 per acre for the 100 acres, their total land investment would be $20,000. An individual share would cost each fisherman $2,000. If this seems expensive, consider these points. Rarely can an individual or a group lose money in land investment. Chances are, the worth of the land will increase, possibly double, over a 10-year period. A shareholder arrangement, where equal amounts of money are paid, works well. If a member wants out of pond ownership, he can sell his share. In a group arrangement, money spent for land can be considered a good investment.

The number of acres purchased can vary according to suitable land available, the number of fishing partners, and the amount that they are willing to invest in recreation. For example, 50 acres of land, having the potential of three four-acre ponds, would cost 10 fishermen $1,000 apiece based on the price of $200 per acre. In reality each man would thus own a five-acre share at $200 per acre.

A smaller group arrangement may be desired. Five men may get together to purchase 50 acres at $200 per acre. They would end up paying $2000 each for the 50-acre parcel. Knowing that land prices can only increase and realizing that the addition of one or more ponds on the land will increase the real estate value, this group of sportsmen will have made a potentially good investment.

Consider also that other improvements could be made to the land to further increase its worth. A well could be drilled, a sewage system installed, fencing and landscaping added, etc. Improvements are investments. They increase real estate value.

If the cost of land seems high, consider the purchase price

of a new automobile. Today's full sized models start at $4000
and rise steadily according to degrees of luxury and options.
Car merchants do not boast that a new car depreciates $600 the
minute it is driven from the dealer's lot, yet cars steadily decline
in value. Some tab this as "planned obsolescence," but a piece
of real estate is nearly immune from such devaluation.

An alternative to land purchase is leasing, but this is an inferior choice. An agreement to allow constructing the pond
must be included in the lease. True pond ownership, however,
is then up for grabs and in the event the lessor should move
or die, problems could arise. The pond developer who leases
land is at the mercy of the landowner. And as most cases
confirm in rental or leasing situations, the pond developer and
user is paying money out rather than investing it. If he has to
move out of the area, the money sunk into land leasing may,
for the most part, be lost and the pond—built at his expense
—left to weeds.

On the other hand, the owner of both pond and land can
sell the land (considering added pond value) and realize some
return on the investment. In a way it very much resembles the
difference between renting and owning a house. Some families
move continually. Economically, they may be better off renting.
But purchasing a house and realizing some financial return
in the event it must be sold is the sounder investment.

A would-be pond developer and operator should consider
leasing the pond site only if there is no other alternative. And
if it comes to that, it may be better not to build the pond at
all.

Remember, too, that by purchasing an adequate number of
acres, an individual or group is investing in a total recreation
area—not just fishing. Consider the other possibilities of such
property. The pond owner is buying a retreat—a place to fish,
swim, possibly hunt, observe wildlife, camp, picnic or just plain
loaf. How much value should you place on such a hideaway?
Such places are rare today—and they are becoming rarer. So
consider the value of such land and the recreation it can afford
when evaluating the investment price.

One of the pleasant features of fish pond ownership is that
it creates landowners from persons who may have never before

considered owning their own chunk of nature. The feeling is a satisfying one and well worth the price.

While land purchase ordinarily is the major financial investment, consider also the construction costs and materials in planning. One may also want to project the costs of second fish plantings, fertilizing, landscaping, fencing and other investments. It is wise to consider all foreseeable costs before construction starts. Most of them can be nailed down to give a reasonable estimate of the total cost of pond ownership.

CONSTRUCTION

Pond owners I talked with estimated their construction costs, which included labor and materials, in the range of from $600 to $2500. This variance reflects the size of different ponds, soil conditions, and different costs of labor and materials. Since costs are changing everyday, and are mainly on the upswing, let's use $2000 for an average cost of a pond. Combine this with the cost of 50 acres of land at $200 an acre and the total comes to $12,000. This is a bit steep for many individuals. But chances are individual pond owners will require less acreage. For example, $400 per acre for 10 acres of land suitable for a pond might be a fair price. This considers the cost per acre increasing with less acres purchased. In some areas, though, cost per acre would be lower. But in this case the individual would be investing $4000 in land and $2000 in construction and labor, for a total cost of $6000. Not far from the prices of some new cars—yet a permanent investment that would increase in value.

Back to the group of fishermen. They may project a total land and construction cost of $12,000. That means ten of them will pay shares of $1200 each. For a nearly complete fishing world, still a good investment at the price.

If you have wondered why specific construction costs, including labor and materials are here omitted, it is because prices vary so much, hence trying to derive specific pond costs would be impractical and deceiving. Rather than try to list exact costs, consider how construction costs are derived. From this you can use the information perhaps to approximate building expenses in your locale.

The Engineering News Record, in the magazine's September, 1972, issue, published a CONSTRUCTION COST INDEX. This index measures the current average cost of labor and materials in various cities throughout the United States. It serves as a comparison figure for construction costs from city to city and from year to year. It is computed using 1913 as the base year when the construction and materials cost index was 100.

Construction cost is based on employee wages, availability of materials, cost of materials, number of workers, amount and type of construction and labor union strength. Here are some comparisons of geographically scattered states, based on the INDEX. Construction costs in Michigan are 33 percent higher than in Colorado. They are eight percent higher than California, 36 percent higher than Louisiana and nine percent higher than Kansas.

In California, costs are 26 percent higher than in Colorado and 30 percent higher than Louisiana.

Wages seem to have the strongest bearing on construction costs. For example, in Michigan, wages are 16 percent higher than in Colorado, three percent higher than California, 13 percent higher than Louisiana and 20 percent lower than Kansas.

Construction costs in June 1972 indicated that California's costs were 10 percent over national average cost; Colorado costs, 20 percent under the national average; Kansas costs, nine percent over the national average; Louisiana costs, 22 percent under the national average and Michigan costs, 15 percent over the national average.

Again, it appears that wages reflect construction costs, along with the other variables mentioned. Here are some typical shovel-tractor (fish pond equipment) labor-wage rates, indicative of August, 1972. They are figured on dollar-per-hour scale. In California, a tractor-shovel operator makes $7.45 an hour; the same job in Colorado pays $6.20; in Florida, the job pays $7.46; in Kansas, the job pays $9.08; in Louisiana, the job pays $7.22; in Michigan, it pays $9.31, and in Oregon, a tractor-shovel operator makes $8.90 per hour.

It seems reasonable to assume that both wages and material

(SCS)

Tractor and heavy equipment operator costs vary from state to state.

costs will increase, therefore construction costs may be expected to rise accordingly.

The INDEX gives an indication of construction costs in your area. SCS technicians and registered engineers in your locale can present the most accurate specific costs based on the size, design and materials that would go into your pond. The scale was presented merely to depict the measures of construction pricing and explain why certain expenses are incurred.

You may, of course, be qualified as a tractor, shovel, dragline, backhoe or boom operator, yourself. Possibly you have a friend in the construction business who will lend a helping hand and/or a piece of equipment. If this is the case, construction costs can be cut in half. But for those not familiar with the equipment, it is advisable to hire an operator.

From plans approved by the SCS or registered engineer, construction personnel will clear and level the area, slope sides, supply and install trickle tube, drainpipe, spillway and inlet and construct the dam. Leveling or grading of the pond area may also be part of the contract. Some companies clear trees and brush. And others can build fences. Any extras requiring heavy equipment operators should be considered, too, at the time of pond planning.

Figure the cost and possible savings through do-it-yourself projects. The conservation and beautification measures to be undertaken make up a significant part of the cost. Local nurseries can help figure cost of sod or grass seed along with suitable trees and shrubs. If you build your own fence, just figure in the cost of material.

A small homemade or commercially-built shed is handy at the pond area. In it can be stored a grass mower, tools, fertilizer platforms, floating dock, fertilizer, fish receiving containers, burlap, aerators, pumps, minnow seines and fish traps, small boat, fishing gear, charcoal grill, charcoal and lighter, picnic and camping supplies and other gear useful to the area.

This is also the time to figure in costs of any recommended water pumps, aerators, stocking containers. Your SCS technician will have specific prices on these items.

POND MANAGEMENT

If your pond qualifies for the Bureau of Sport Fisheries and Wildlife stocking, as it should under SCS guidance, the first stocking will be free of charge. A warm water pond may not need a second stocking, but a trout pond needs regular stocking.

Subsequent stocking is purchased from private hatcheries. Trout usually cost about $15 for 1,000 fry. Or one to three cents an inch for fingerlings up to four inches. And $40 per 1,000 small fingerlings. Some hatcheries also ask a delivery charge. The cost is about $20 per surface acre to stock a pond annually.

Fertilization costs run about $25 to $50 a surface acre for one year. A rough estimate would be 1,000 pounds of 8-8-0 inorganic fertilizer per acre each year. By fertilizing on a regular basis, the cost of fertilizer offsets the cost of herbicides that would be needed to control unwanted aquatic vegetation.

Commercial fish raising operations have the additional cost of feed for fish. But the private fish pond owner usually omits feeding and eliminates the cost of pelleted fish food.

(SCS)

By sharing expenses a group of sportsmen can develop their own fish pond. Another possibility might be to lease an existing older pond and improve its fishing.

A TYPICAL ACCOUNT

His name wasn't necessarily Ike Walton, but here's his account:

*   *   *   *   *

My name is Ike Walton. I wanted a fish pond. I live in the suburbs of Detroit, Michigan, and was tired of fighting the fishing pressure. Besides, I wanted a place for me and my family and some close friends.

Nine of my buddies were also interested in a fish pond. A couple of them belonged to my church. One of them was a longtime fishing partner. And some of my fellow workers at the mill were excited about it, too. We started making plans.

There were 50 acres of land for sale not far from home.

A small stream ran through the property and the SCS technician I visited said the property would make a good pond and recreation site.

So the ten of us purchased the 50 acres of land. At $200 per acre we each paid $1,000. In the spring of the year, after consulting with the SCS and game and fish department, we planned the fish pond. We decided to build one three-acre pond with hopes of adding more ponds if the first one worked out. Each of us chipped in an additional $300 to cover the cost of construction (high in Michigan), labor and all the materials recommended by the SCS.

We also took into consideration taxes on the land. The annual fees would be divided amongst us. Our taxes ran higher close to the city than those further from home. Also, we fully realized our land tax rates were subject to change. It is a good idea to find out tax rates on land with water sources, ponds or other improvements, before purchasing.

The pond was finished and stocked late in the spring with bass and bluegill by the Bureau of Sport Fisheries. The stocking was free. We bought $60 worth of fertilizer. After the pond was filled and stocked, we fertilized the water.

On the weekends we all got together, sometimes with our families, and worked on the pond area. There were trees to be cleared close to the bank. Grass was planted and sod laid in areas on the dam and around the shoreline. Our local total outlay was $25 here.

A couple of us had extra mowers. After clearing the deadfall and shrubs we sickled the weeds low and mowed them.

We planted new trees—pines and oaks. And added some hedges and shrubs that were recommended by a local conservation officer. By the time summer was over, we even had a pole fence built with a wooden gate that locked. Each family was given a key and used the pond area at will. Fishing was out of the question until the third spring—two years after planting. But I think we used our land every weekend, anyway.

The kids helped us with seining operations. All of us enjoyed checking on the bass and bluegill. The planting had taken hold and the fish were growing fast. We fertilized again the next year. And the close attention we gave the pond really paid off, Only a few weeds grew.

On June 1 most of the families met at the pond. It was opening day for us. We caught enough bass and bluegill for the best fish fry I can remember. And that evening, after we had pitched tents on a small knoll overlooking the pond, I counted all the blessings that 50 acres of land and three acres full of bass and bluegill gave us. I think that is when I started thinking about a second pond. (And the following year it became reality). Ten fishing families had contributed a total of $1,308.50 (this figure does not include annual land taxes . . . subject to change, nor does it include minor expenditures that vary from pond to pond and area to area) each for a part of a fishing-camping treasure . . . the price of a used car or a motor boat. The pond has given us a multitude of joys, as it will give our sons and daughters. A small price to pay for a place of our own.

7 | Fish Stocking

IN THE PRECEDING CHAPTERS IT WAS MENTIONED THAT THE STOCKING rates are dependent on available food in the pond, size of the fish desired and how many fish are harvested from the pond. Also discussed were the reasons why certain species of sport fish are stocked. Cold water and warm water ponds are stocked according to size of the pond, depth, climate and species of available fish that thrive in the area.

Stocking a pond is similar to a farmer planting seed. The fields have been prepared. The soil is in good condition. And the rich earth is ready to accept seeds. How well the fields have been tilled, how rich the soil, how the farmer plants the seeds, and the management thereafter will determine how bountiful the harvest. So it is with fish ponds. Planning and construction have been completed. The pond is filled. After three days or so the water has settled to relative clarity. And the fish are ready to be planted.

Before actually releasing cold or warm water fingerlings into a pond, a stocking plan is created for the pond owner. No two ponds are alike. Each pond's stocking formula is unique. And the local SCS technician and fisheries biologist works out the plan.

STOCKING COLD WATER SPECIES

Stocking a cold water trout pond is rather simple. For best fishing, plant trout, but only trout fingerlings. Rarely does satisfying fishing occur when trout and some other species such as perch, walleye or northern pike are planted together. Unlike warm water ponds where several species of fish can exist together with a reasonable degree of population balance, trout do best by themselves.

Rainbow trout is the most common choice for stocking ponds. It thrives under a wide range of conditions, grows fast, and is more disease resistant. Rainbows are more widely available from hatcheries than other kinds of trout. The brook trout is favored in the East, but is more sensitive to temperature change than other trout. In some sections of the country, rainbow and brook are planted together for variety. Whether they are stocked together or singly is a matter of choice.

One may wonder why other types of trout, namely browns and cutthroats, are not suitable for fish ponds. The main reason is that relatively few hatcheries in the country have them available for private stocking. Little is known about the cutthroat under fish pond conditions, but the brown has proven itself inadequate. The brown trout lives longer than other trout and grows large in ponds but is cannibalistic and harder to catch.

In New England some stocking plans have proven ideal for recreational fishing. Biologists in these states agree that 600 trout fingerlings an acre can be planted for top fishing. Brook trout is a popular species and produces a high catch in the spring. Rainbow trout produces a lower catch in these areas with the best fishing coming in the summer. A combination of brook and rainbow in a New England pond produces the longest fishing season.

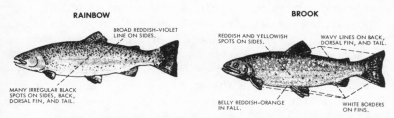

RAINBOW

BROAD REDDISH-VIOLET
LINE ON SIDES.

MANY IRREGULAR BLACK
SPOTS ON SIDES, BACK,
DORSAL FIN, AND TAIL.

BROOK

REDDISH AND YELLOWISH
SPOTS ON SIDES.

WAVY LINES ON BACK,
DORSAL FIN, AND TAIL.

BELLY REDDISH-ORANGE
IN FALL.

WHITE BORDERS
ON FINS.

Rainbow and brook trout are best suited for cold water ponds.

Trout fingerlings, two to four inches long, are the best to stock in a cold water pond. They are available initially from the Bureau of Sport Fisheries and Wildlife upon pond qualification. Fingerlings are recommended over advanced fry whose size usually ranges from one to two inches, usually too small for survival. Fisheries experts estimate a natural mortality rate among fingerlings during the first year of the pond as 10 to 20 percent, while fry in a new pond would have a rate ranging from 30 to 50 percent. In most cases, depending on availability from the hatchery, trout are stocked in the spring.

(SCS)

Fingerlings being netted from planting truck.

Stocking a pond with catchable size trout is not only more expensive, but the mortality rate is higher than with fingerlings. As explained earlier, when the fish in a pond reach a certain poundage or carrying capacity, they begin to decline. Almost immediately upon stocking, catchable-size trout show high mortality. And although the waiting period from the time of stocking to the time of fishing would be eliminated, their stocking would have to be repeated too frequently—once a year at least, and depending on the amount of fishing, maybe even twice.

Instant fishing, created by the introduction of catchables into a pond, appears at first to be the quickest way to good fishing. But it isn't. It does not offer good fishing in the long run. The satisfaction of seeing fish grow big, fat and healthy is also missed. And planting easily caught, catchable fish closely resembles the stocking programs typical of put-and-take fee-pond operators and some done in public waters by state conservation agencies. Fish raised from fingerlings and grown to catchable size in a pond have a degree of wildness about them that rivals many virgin lakes and streams. Ordinarily they are stronger and healthier than catchable fish moved from one

(SCS)

Fish should be gently released into pond after making sure water temperature of container and pond water is similar.

habitat to another and then expected to adapt immediately to the new.

When fingerling trout are planted initially, the need for restocking occurs only every two or three years unless there is a gravel bottomed stream with clean running water favorable for trout spawning.

Before restocking trout for the first time, the best method is to remove existing fish. Hopefully this can be done by fishing, but chemical treatment may be needed. If it can't be done this way, drain the pond and remove the fish the fishermen were unable to catch. If some big fish are left in the pond after restocking, they usually become cannibalistic and are apt to drastically reduce the number of newly planted fingerlings.

Although stocking experts have approximated the fish capacity of certain ponds, the pond owner also is instrumental in determining accurate stocking numbers. Records of removal, growth and survival should be kept by the owner. After a couple of seasons, best stocking rates will be determined. Variables in pond stocking can change according to the fertility of pond water. Record keeping forms are available from SCS.

It is interesting to note that in Idaho a good stocking formula has been developed by keeping accurate records. Without any supplemental feeding (typical of ponds used primarily for sport fishing) a one-acre pond could be stocked with 400 to 500 fingerlings when four-ounce trout were desired the first year. But 300 to 400 fingerlings are stocked if six-ounce fish are wanted. Or 200 to 300 trout are stocked if eight-ounce fish are the objective. This is a general rule and certain waters vary in production.

There are a few general points to remember about trout stocking procedure. Avoid stocking trout in water above 65 degrees F. Keep in mind that trout are sensitive to sudden changes in temperature, oxygen, carbon dioxide, alkalinity or acidity. For these reasons trout should not be dumped directly from the fish container into the pond. Instead pond water should be added slowly to the water in the shipping container until it is within six degrees F. of the temperature of the pond water. One way to do this is to pour out half the water from the container. Place the container in the pond and pour pond water slowly into it.

Mixing container water with water where trout are to be planted is important.

When it is full, pour out about half the mixture and repeat the process twice.

If the trout show signs of distress such as turning on their sides, delay the mixing technique until they act normally. After mixing, pour the fingerlings gently into the pond.

Fish delivery procedure varies in many states. A pond owner should be prepared to receive fingerlings at a predetermined meeting point. Part of the equipment needed are clean con-

(SCS)

Meeting the planting truck at a predetermined time is important.

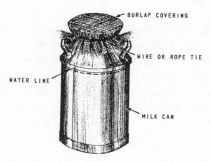

Milk can with burlap cover is best for transporting fish.

tainers, partially filled with cool, unchlorinated water for transporting the fish. Water from city systems is usually chlorinated
and will kill fish. Anti-chlorination tablets are available from
aquarium shops. Hatchery containers are not loaned to pond
owners for stocking. Milk cans work well, provided the covers
are left off and replaced with covers of porous material. Burlap
makes a good covering. So does cheesecloth. Cut to an appropriate size, the cover can be securely tied around the lip of
the can.

Fish should be taken immediately to the water in which they
will be planted. During transport, water in the containers is
usually agitated enough to restore some oxygen by splashing.
If not, oxygen depletion could kill some fish. Rough roads ordinarily do not harm the fish provided there is enough water in
the container. The notification card sent by the hatchery informs
pond owners how much water to bring. The quantity of water
suggested usually keeps fish alive and well for one hour under
good transport conditions.

If travel is over a smooth road during transport and little or
no splashing takes place, check the fish frequently. If they rise
to the surface and appear to be gasping, oxygen should be restored. This can be done by dipping the water and letting it
fall from a height of about two feet. Repeat the process two or
three times every few minutes. Unattended fish or fish left
overnight in containers have a slim chance of survival. Containers should be sheltered from the sun to prevent the water

from heating. Should the water become considerably warmer than it was at the time of transfer from the stocking truck, a small chunk of ice can be placed above the container. Wrapping the cans in wet sacking during periods of hot weather will also keep the temperatures more uniform. At the release site, scatter the fish as widely as possible adjacent to deep or protected areas.

A good, general formula for the number of trout to be stocked takes into account amount of water surface area and its fertility proportionate to the pond's quality of water and length of fish growing season.

STOCKING WARM WATER SPECIES

Due to the mixing of warm water species, mostly largemouth bass and sunfish, in warm water ponds, a stocking sequence is followed. Although appearing complicated at first glance, the order is rather simple. The sequence is based on spawning habits and the ecological relationships of the various species of fish used in fish ponds.

For example, the sunfish family (bluegill and redear sunfish) are stocked during the fall and winter months. Largemouth bass are stocked during the spring following the introduction of bluegill or redear sunfish. (There are local nicknames for members of the sunfish family, such as bream, brim (bluegills) or shell-cracker (redears), pumpkinseeds or sunnies, but only nationally recognized fish nomenclature is used here for the sake of clarity.)

Stocking rates vary according to states. In South Carolina for example, an established rate of 400 sunfish and 300 largemouth bass fingerlings per surface acre are stocked. Ponds in Arkansas, Florida, Georgia, Louisiana, Maryland, Mississippi, North Carolina, Tennessee and Virginia are stocked at the rate of 500 sunfish and 50 largemouth bass fingerlings per surface acre.

The stocking rates for channel catfish are 50 per acre in combinations with bass and sunfish or 100 per acre in catfish-only ponds.

In a few instances approval may be granted for higher stocking rates in some ponds. The recommendation of a fishery

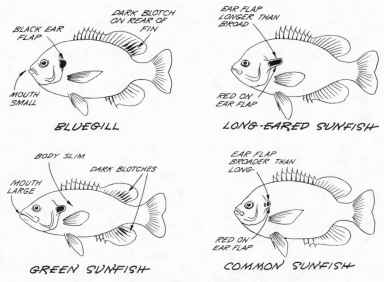

Various species of bluegill and sunfish can be stocked.

biologist, in conjunction with the approval of a regional Bureau of Sport Fisheries office is needed. Criteria for granting this approval is based on the pond owner's thorough understanding of established pond fertilization methods and his ability to manage the pond accordingly. (Fertilization will be discussed in detail in Chapter 11—Pond Management).

As is the case with trout, warm water fish in fingerling size are stocked by the Bureau of Sport Fisheries. Fry, from one to two inches, suffer a high mortality rate in warm water ponds. And catchable fish plantings are discouraged for the same reasons mentioned in trout stocking.

In the New England states, largemouth bass are considered the favored warm water game fish. Stocked as fingerlings in a well fertilized pond, they will attain a growth of about 10 inches in one year, and they are able to spawn in two years. In these states, bass are usually stocked in combination with minnows, especially golden shiners. The addition of this forage fish adds good size and poundage to bass, Without them, the poundage of harvestable fish is considerably less. New England biologists concur that despite the good growth of bass, intensive sound management in their areas is needed for long lasting, good fishing.

It is interesting to note that in the New England states game and fish departments put heavy restrictions on the importation and stocking of bluegill. They are used as forage fish with satisfactory results, but their numbers are kept closely curtailed.

Bluegill are not looked down upon by fisheries biologists. But sunfish population balance is difficult to maintain. Stocking them together with a predator fish, such as bass, provides a degree of control, if they are adequately harvested along with the bass. On the other hand, stocking of bluegills by themselves in a pond would result in the water being overpopulated with small fish. This is especially true after the sunfish have spawned several times. Adding more fish does not help.

In most ponds when bass are stocked alone the result has been relatively low poundages of harvestable fish. Forage fish, minnows or small bluegills, are food necessary for bass and the largemouth has proven to be the most satisfactory warm water game fish for stocking fish ponds.

In South Dakota, stocking rates vary from those used in southern warm water ponds. In South Dakota, for instance, 100 bass fingerlings and 300 bluegill fingerlings are stocked for each surface acre of water. Both species are stocked initially in a time period extending from June through August. The fish are harvested after the bass have successfully reproduced, and no repeat stocking is recommended while the fish population is in balance.

By comparing northern and southern warm water states, it is apparent that there is a variation in stocking rates. It is important to realize that different areas have different rates. Missouri, for instance, located in the country's mid-section, has tried other stocking methods.

Two different methods of stocking fish ponds were evaluated in Missouri. In 1962, 52 ponds were stocked with largemouth bass in the summer and bluegill and channel catfish in the fall (the first method). The ponds were then test-seined in 1965. In 1966, comparative data was collected from 41 ponds that were stocked with all three species simultaneously in the fall of 1963 (the second method). Criteria for evaluation included population structure and growth rates of fish populations.

The results? Stocking methods had little effect on the sizes attained by the various year classes of bass, bluegill and channel cats. Differences in growth and the average total length of the fish from the different stocking methods were usually less than one inch.

Ponds stocked by the first method appeared to have better fish population structures than when all three species were planted simultaneously. This assumes, however, that none of the pond owners using the first stocking method were negligent in stocking bluegills.

The results of the stocking tests show that in Missouri, at least, stocking sequence (summer and fall) is not essential to fish growth since little difference in fish length between the two methods was found. However, population structure, or desirable balance among bass, bluegills and channel cats was better by following the spring-fall sequence. Maintaining a good popuation structure in a fish pond environment is of extreme importance to the pond owner. Therefore, despite the same size growth, the spring-fall sequence remains the best method.

The success of stocking warm water ponds is dependent on the same general criteria as for success in cold water stocking. Temperature, water quality, oxygen, acidity, alkalinity and muddiness have important effects on management of warm water species. Fish in warm water ponds grow best in water temperatures above 65 degrees F. Healthy fish need a good supply of oxygen. This they obtain from the water by way of its surface absorption from the air and by microscopic plants through photosynthesis. Excess acidity, alkalinity and water muddiness can cause poor growth of newly stocked fish. (More about this in Chapter 11.)

Intensive management is the key to successful warm water fish pond management. With the proper mixture of fish, a good population balance is obtained. Drastic imbalances result from promiscuous stocking or planting species of fish not manageable under fish pond conditions. A pond owner, for example, may catch some bullheads from a lake and stock them in his pond, yet the introduction of the bullheads could disrupt his whole population of bass and bluegill. The pond owner can make the same mistake with bass and bluegill. Larger fish of these species could be caught from another source and released in the fish pond. Without understanding the total concept of fish balance, the owner thus creates an imbalance that could ruin the fishing and make pond restocking necessary.

There are certain species of warm water fish that are difficult to manage in the fish pond. Among them, perch and crappie have been unsuccessfully tried by pond owners. Perch, like sunfish, are prolific breeders. Even in large lakes and rivers their numbers are often stunted due to overpopulation. But in smaller ponds they are nearly impossible to control. And, unlike bluegill, yellow perch are cannibalistic and can wipe out other species in the pond. Perch in the four or five inch class—too small for fishing fun or eating—are particularly fond of bass, bluegill and even trout fingerlings.

One of the goals of the fish pond manager should be to keep the water level of the pond fairly stable. This aids bass and bluegill spawning. Crappie, however, cannot be successfully managed in ponds that have uniform water levels all year. They do well in some irrigation reservoirs and lakes that fluctuate significantly in surface area. One result of this fluctuation is that a low water level in summer restricts crappie reproduction. They are otherwise prolific breeders, of course. But the larger surface area in winter and spring, with its greater food supply, allows the surviving crappie to grow rapidly to usable size. Hence, it is not impossible to manage good crappie fishing. Some states, like Kansas, yield good fish pond catches. But the management has to be extremely tough. For the individual pond owner or sportsmen's group, bass and bluegill would provide better fishing with more time to enjoy it.

Carp are preferred by some. In the Midwest, carp ponds offer good recreation. The degree of sport involved in fishing for carp is, of course, a matter of individual taste. They can be fun to catch on light spinning or fly rod outfits. But rarely do they take artificial baits. And carp (although eaten and enjoyed by some) leave something to be desired on the dinner table as

Due to their predator nature bass can help check overpopulation. Perch (right, above) are fine gamefish, but considered a poor species to stock. Some trout, like the brown (lower left) are too cannibalistic for fish ponds. Bass and bluegill (lower right) are the kings of the warm water ponds.

compared to bass, bluegill and trout. Carp are prolific breeders. They are regarded as rough fish by most sport fishing enthusiasts. And, their bottom feeding habits have muddied many good bass and bluegill ponds. The stocking of carp, either by themselves or with other species of fish, is not recommended.

Some populations of bait fish—minnows—aid fish growth in warm water ponds. The local fisheries biologist and SCS technician can advise whether or not to stock bait or forage fish. Warm water ponds used exclusively to produce bait fish are not designed and managed in the same way as ponds for fishing. (More about raising bait fish, however, in Chapter 9— Making Money.)

As mentioned earlier, bullheads stocked in fish ponds usually cause problems. Although they afford fine recreational fishing in public lakes and streams and are a delight on the table, bullheads are rarely managed successfully under pond conditions. In a few areas, they have been grown successfully by stocking a pond after their reproduction season is over. They are then harvested the next spring before they can reproduce again. Overpopulation causes stunting in bullhead populations, too.

In regards to warm water fish delivery, transport and actual stocking procedures, follow the general rules already mentioned for cold water stocking. Warm water species are somewhat hardier. But getting them to the pond in the shortest time and then releasing them gently will add to stocking success. Clean containers are essential and their oxygen requirements must be met.

For stocking both cold and warm water species, some state conservation agencies require stocking permits. The fisheries or SCS technician will advise whether such a permit is needed. Think of this permit as a worthwhile attempt by state game and fish departments to keep a careful check on the number of fish ponds in their state. It also keeps them up-to-date on correct stocking procedures. There have been times in the past when indiscriminate stocking—both as to methods and species of fish planted—have caused serious threats to public fishing waters.

In this chapter, the pond owner has introduced underwater life to his pond. This is the beginning of good fishing. In a year or two, he will reap the harvest of his efforts. The care and devotion he gives the pond while the fish are growing to catchable size will determine how good the fishing will be.

8 | Pond Fishing

A PLEASING ASPECT OF POND FISHING IS KNOWING THAT THE MORE fish are harvested, the more the pond is fished, the better the fishing will be. Catching fish is an important part of pond management. And in order to maintain balance of fish populations in the pond, fish it as much as possible.

This theory is hard to accept by some anglers. They have been taught to throw the small ones back. They have also been taught that catching and releasing fish is a philosophy of the true sportsman when, in fact, the theory has actually ruined some good fishing holes.

The catch-and-release theory, so popular with some anglers today, has some holes in it. Fish have remarkable powers of renewing their numbers. In the warm water class, bluegill are so prolific that managing them is tough. In cold water, brook trout breed to the extent that many brookie streams and ponds are filled with stunted fish. According to Jack Walstrom, biologist with the SCS in Kansas, "a good fish pond requires from 300 to 500 manhours of fishing effort per acre, per year, to keep fish production at the optimum level. Research has shown that it is virtually impossible to 'fish out' a pond by hook and line methods."

Throwing the small ones (four to six inches long) back "to grow up and be caught later" is a noble idea. But fisheries experts agree it is one that violates good fish management. In fish ponds, especially, small fish should be harvested along with the big ones. A good rule to follow is anything big enough to eat should be kept. There is nothing cruel or unsportsmanlike about harvesting small prolific-breeding fish. It is doing the overall fish population a service. When the small fish are harvested, more food is available for those remaining. Fish will grow faster and the ones then caught will be bigger.

Fred Eiserman, a good friend who coordinates the fisheries program in Wyoming, disagrees with the current emphasis on catch-and-release programs on public waters. As he puts it, a certain percentage of fish population must be harvested in order to have good fishing.

The secret to good fishing, he says, is habitat. When the fish populations have clean, unpolluted, nutrient-rich waters, they reproduce amazingly fast. To reach a balance of good fish growth and health, certain numbers must be harvested. If they are not harvested, stunting and fish die-offs can occur. Poor fish habitat, *not* fishing pressure, creates poor fishing.

Some of the finest trout streams in the country are subject to pressure from various groups. They want to control fisherman pressure by various techniques. Fly-fishing-only, catch and release, regulating the size and number limits and length of season have been tried. Some regulations are needed and do some good. But anglers should keep the fish they catch. If a two-pound rainbow trout is taken from a productive trout stream, another big fish will replace it. Harvest is vital to the stream.

What about the theory that a lake or stream is all fished out? Or that fishing is getting too tough because of all the competition? Several factors are responsible for poor overall fishing.

The habitat of the water may not be as good as it was in "the good old days." Fish get smarter? Not enough *good* fishermen are fishing the water. And stocking techniques may have fallen off. Variable factors also affect fishing—season, weather, temperature and time of day. These factors, taken into consideration by good fishermen, are used to their advantage.

Harvesting a portion of the fish population in a given pond can be compared to big-game hunting management techniques. There are a certain number of animals that X-number of habitat acres can support. Depending on the quality of that habitat, game managers know that numbers above the normal population cannot be supported. Therefore a specified number of hunting permits are issued to thin the herd. Hunting success, although many times dependent on the same factors involved in fishing, can be forecast accurately enough from past seasons to assure the desired harvest.

Since man has devoured thousands of acres of wildlife habitat, the game management tool is the only reasonable way of insuring balance among game herds. It is interesting to note that both game bird and game animal numbers have grown or remained steady since the advent of modern game management principles. Harvesting a portion of the herd according to the carrying capacity of the land is the real reason for success. The need for fishing harvest is similar.

Game animal numbers allowed to go beyond the carrying capacity of the land due to insufficient harvest can result in drastic herd losses. There is no reasonable system of sharing, as we know it, among game animals. When the available food contained in 100 acres of winter mule deer range is depleted, the deer die or must move elsewhere. In many areas, however, man has blocked or eliminated their natural migration routes by fences and roads. Many game herds are thus prevented from finding new ranges. The sight of 60 or 70 head of deer dead from starvation is not a pleasant one, but it happens.

Hunting and fishing have lots in common. But one does not have to be a hunter or even enjoy the sport to see the necessity for harvest. And harvest is the key to good fishing in the pond. Keep those lines wet!

WHEN TO START

In a cold water pond, start fishing for trout one year after stocking. The fingerlings planted will be around six to eight inches long by then, provided food has been plentiful.

For warm water ponds, the second year after stocking marks the maximum pounds of fish developed and possible based on the fertility level maintained. Begin fishing bass and bluegills when the bass have reproduced. This ordinarily occurs the first spring after they are stocked if they mature correctly.

To be sure of successful propogation, run a minnow seine along the edge of the pond. If no one or two-inch bass are taken in the seine, the pond stocking was unsuccessful. It would then be best to restock with bass immediately, using the same stocking rate as with a new pond. The fisheries technician may recommend first killing the remaining original fish in the pond before restocking.

Fish the bass lightly for the first two or three months after they have spawned. It is important not to fish the bluegills until after the bass have spawned for the first time. The first spawn of bass maintains predation pressure on subsequent bluegill spawns and consequently these bass tend to relieve fishing pressure on the original bass stock.

Channel cats can be fished when they weigh 10 to 12 ounces, which is usually a year after they are stocked.

After the bass have spawned, begin fishing the bluegills. In some states, pond managers have found they can obtain a desirable balance of bass and bluegill when they catch 15 bluegills for each bass. In Colorado, the SCS recommends harvesting about four pounds of bluegills for each pound of bass to maintain proper balance between bass and bluegill.

THE POND'S CARRYING CAPACITY

As is the case with game animals in their habitat, the fish pond also has a carrying capacity—a point where fish numbers match the availability of water and food. Fingerling trout reach this point one year from the time they are stocked. In warm water ponds the capacity is reached two years after stocking. Beyond this point fish growth slows almost to a stop and the number of fish and their poundage also decreases. The natural loss rate removes fish faster than they can grow; most fish have only a two year life span. It is for this reason that fish catching, harvesting the fish and maintaining fishing pressure is the ultimate goal of fish ponding.

It is not hard to understand why overstocking produces fish stunting and increases their mortality rates, while understocking .results in larger fish. The level of carrying capacity in any fish pond is just so much. Reaching it is inevitable. Harvesting the fish maintains the balance needed for good fishing.

In a cold water fish pond most original trout will be gone by the third year. Also, only in rare exceptions do trout reproduce in fish ponds. David Allan, New Hampshire SCS biologist, says that in some ponds in his state trout reproduction has been possible through SCS spawning area development. Trout need shallow, gravel-bottomed, flowing streams to spawn. Otherwise it is necessary to stock the pond with fingerlings every two years.

Warm water species are capable of reproducing in fish ponds, making subsequent stockings unnecessary. But this is possible only when a balance of fish is maintained. Neglect by pond owners is the major reason why warm water ponds eventually need to be restocked.

If numerous yearling bass weighing less than a half pound are being caught in the spring of any year, there are too many. Keep the fish caught. The others will grow larger.

Bluegill and redear sunfish that have not spawned can be stimulated to do so by fishing them harder or by fertilizing. The best fishing for them seems to be over their spawning beds. This will not upset the bass-bluegill balance in the pond.

For the best bass fishing, an angler should fish the usable size sunfish as well. Consider even a two-ounce bluegill or redear sunfish as usable. A six-ounce bass should also be considered as usable and be kept, for all fishing will not be rewarded with large fish at first.

Small fish in the pond may be considered bass up to four inches and sunfish up to two and a half inches. Large bass depend on these fish as food, so steady production of small fish means rapid growth and heavier poundage for bass.

A pond that provides good fishing usually has 60 percent or more of its total poundage in usable fish. If more than 30 percent of a pond's total poundage is in the three to five inch intermediate-size sunfish, fishing is usually poor.

Correcting an overpopulation of intermediate-size bluegills purely through trying to fish them out is difficult. The best way to correct the situation might be to use a 50 or 60-foot, one-half inch mesh seine and pass it through the shallow parts of the pond. Sort out the usables and throw back those big enough for fishing. Destroy smaller sunfish. A pond should be seined about every ten days until most of the sunfish caught are of usable size. Sometimes seining may not be feasible. The fish may have to be killed and the pond restocked. (See Chapter 11.) Small bass, on the other hand, can usually be caught and fished out.

CATCHING TROUT

The fruits of the pond owner's planning and labor can now be fully realized. The trout in his pond may be the fattest, spunkiest specimens he has ever set a hook into. The fishing could be the best he has ever enjoyed.

The catching should be easy during the first several outings, just as fishing is fast in newly stocked public waters. But the trout will grow wise—fast. And then the real fun begins. If fishing was consistently easy, we all would soon tire of it. Remember that the moods and feeding habits of the pond fish are subject to the same variables as wild fish. Time of year, time of day, water temperature, barometer—all are factors. So is the fisherman's ability.

Trout such as the rainbow or brook have favorite foods. Methods of catching trout differ from warm water fishing. Here are some tips on how to catch them.

Tackle

For trout, keep the gear light. Ultra-light and light-action rods will give more sport, especially when the fish are running small. Light rods allow the use of low test monofilament line in the four to six-pound category. Little or no weight for casting is needed with light line. Smaller baits do not require heavy sinkers and consequently offerings appear more natural-looking to fish.

Open or closed face spinning reels are easy to use. They come in lightweight and ultra-light models designed to be used with lightweight rods. Bait casting reels, although favorites for many warm water and saltwater species, are harder to master and are not used as effective as spinning outfits for trout.

Fly fishing gear, called the ultimate method for catching trout by some, is fun when correct casting techniques are learned. While it takes some time to master a fly rod, the fish pond is a good place to practice. A lightweight, well-balanced outfit is desirable for trout.

Rainbow Trout

Best baits are garden worms, nightcrawlers, grasshoppers, hellgramites, salmon eggs, cheese (soft cheese that could be molded on the hook like Velveeta; garlic-flavored cheese sometimes works well) and marshmallows (small, miniature types) that can be bought in groceries, or those that are sold especially for fishing. Different colors sometimes work good and those with garlic flavor or cheese are deadly at times. Minnows, both live and dead, are good baits. Be careful when using live minnows. They could be rough fish fingerlings that would cause fish pond problems later.

Bait hooks should be small. Rainbow trout have small mouths. Special cheese holders, usually treble hooks, are available and they keep molded bait on best.

A good rule for rainbows when using bait is to use little or no weight. A light fishing outfit will enable you to cast the bait far enough. A splitshot or two can be clamped on the line for more casting distance. An effective method for rainbows anytime of year is to thread a nightcrawler on the hook just through the collar of the worm . . . so that it appears natural. Cast the bait and let it sink naturally. Leave the line loose. Chances are a fish will hit it before the bait reaches the bottom. The line will then tighten and you can set the hook.

If worms aren't working, try other baits. Trout can be tempermental feeders. Experiment to find out what they like. Their taste in foods vary from day to day.

Lures for trout are usually smaller than the traditional bass plugs. But some bass lures work equally well on trout. Small nickel and brass spinners, with or without bucktails, are effective. Small, wobbling spoons work well. And spinner-live worm combinations nail trout. Cast the lure and let it sink close to the bottom. Retrieve with a pumping motion or series of fast jerks.

A general rule for using flies for trout is to fish dry flies early in the morning and late afternoon when the fish are rising. During mid-day hours, wet flies, such as nymphs (those flies, usually weighted, that are tied to look like the bottom organisms that trout feed on) and streamers work best. In general, best colors for flies are brown, black and gray. Small sizes are effective because they more closely match the size of natural insects. Sizes 14 through 18 would fit most types of fishing.

Flies can be fished without the use of a fly rod and still be cast sufficiently to reach feeding fish. The method is called the "Bubble" technique, employed in many western trout states. A clear plastic bubble (similar to a float) is attached to the line. The bubble can be filled with water to add weight for casting or it can be cast by itself. A leader, perhaps a foot or more long, is attached to the bubble. The fly can then be tied directly to the line. The weight of the bubble, when cast, carries the fly to feeding fish. Two types of retrieves work best. In both methods, first let the bubble rest on the water a few seconds. During the first retrieve, wind the line in slowly with regular turns of the handle until the fly reaches the bank. It is important to reel in all the way at this same speed because fish often hit the fly when it is only a few feet from the bank. Some trout will follow a fly for long distances. When they believe it is escaping, they hit it.

The other method is to use a series of erratic line retrieves. Let the fly settle first, then give it a jerk. Let it settle and then repeat the jerk. Continue this type of retrieve until all the line is retrieved.

Set the hook with moderate force. When playing rainbow trout, keep the rod tip up. Rainbows are noted for aerial fighting tactics. They often throw a hook or break the line when the rod tip is down.

Brook Trout

Baits, lures and flies for the rainbow can also be used effectively on brook trout. But there are some special tricks that seem especially effective on this member of the char family. In the live bait category, brookies are more cannibalistic than rainbow trout. Worms and minnows are their favorites while baits like cheese and marshmallows don't interest them much.

Brookies favor spinner blades that feature gaudy colors. Red and white combination blades are good. Blaze orange works well. And solid red is effective. Brookies are especially fond of spinner and worm combinations.

A dash of red or orange seems to drive brook trout crazy. Dry and wet fly patterns, sporting a splash of red on the body, wings or hackle add effectiveness to brook trout flies.

Brookies have a tendency to hit a bait with a series of bumps. When you hook a good one, be ready for a grinding underwater contest. Considered to be one of the top eating of the trouts, the brookies flesh is firm. Its meat is sometimes pinkish-orange color—usually brought about by a diet of fresh water shrimp.

In my experience, brook trout usually hit lures deeper than most rainbows. So let the bait sink till it hits bottom and then begin the retrieve. A jerky one seems best for brook trout.

Ice Fishing

Cold water species like rainbows and brook trout hit well under the ice. If the pond is located where ice cover lasts for a month or two and the ice is safe enough to fish from, you are in for a lot of fun—all the while doing a service to the fish and the pond by harvesting the crop!

Bore or chop a hole in the ice large enough to pull a hooked fish through it. Several holes in various locations are better than one. Fish under the ice are usually congregated at a few desirable locations where food is available. Finding the depth at which the fish are biting is one of the challenges, too, of ice fishing. That's the reason for drilling several holes over various sections of the pond. Set bait at various depths.

Tiny ice jigs or flies are good for catching winter trout. Yellow and orange are good colors. The flies are weighted so they can be jigged up and down.

Jigging spoons and spinners through the ice are potent techniques. Baits like worms, cheese and marshmallows catch trout.

Ice fishermen are sometimes regarded as anglers lacking one or several of their senses. But give the sport a try. It has its own joys and thrills. And it can break the monotony of a long winter otherwise spent in front of a television set.

CATCHING BASS

The hows, whys, whens and whats of largemouth bass fishing have been expounded to such a degree that it would seem Old Bigmouth just doesn't stand a chance anymore. Not so. The largemouth, bigmouth, mossback, linesides, black bass or any name that you care to give this top gamefish, has held its own. Despite electric fish finders, and speedy, modern bass boats, the largemouth can still be as unpredictable and moody as ever. The fisherman stands a good chance of catching lots of bass in his pond. So get ready for fast action.

(SCS)

Rainbow trout and largemouth bass can be caught on a number of baits.

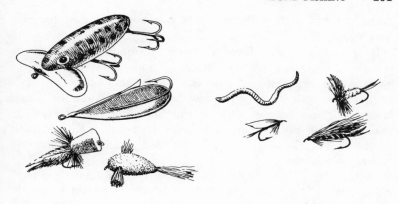

SOME FAVORITES FOR BASS —

TRY THESE FOR BLUEGILLS —

Sample lures which have been successful in warm water ponds.

Tackle

Fishing for largemouths with light tackle is possible and a lot of fun. But a medium-weight spinning outfit is recommended —one with enough backbone to let ol' mossback know you are there. Open or closed faced spin reels can do the job. The choice of experts these days though seems to be the level-wind bait casting reels that have been modernized with anti-backlash devices. They are still not foolproof, but these reels are fun to use for bass from four pounds up. Smaller bass can be handled adequately on spin tackle. The use of a bait casting outfit for bass can be likened to the use of fly rod and reel for trout. They seem to go together. Bass fishermen, like trout fishermen, are not at all as choosy about the type of rod or reel as things like choice of line.

For the spinning outfits, my reels carry six or eight-pound test monofiliment line. Some bassmen would say this is a bit on the light side. But this weight line casts better than heavy mono and means I can use smaller lures.

Bait casting reels seem to work best when spooled with mono or braided nylon in the 10 to 20 pound class. When the big bass in the pond are on the prowl, this would be my choice.

Fly fishing for bass with poppers and hair bugs is fun. Medium to heavy rods with plenty of backbone are best for bug bass fishing.

Largemouths have favorite foods. Minnows, crawfish or crawdads, nightcrawlers rank near the top. They will also inhale frogs, mice, snakes, insects, lizards and other gamefish at times. Some items on the bass menu make impractical baits, however. Minnows seem to be the best live bait. Crawdads will work well during long hot spells when they can be fished off the bottom. Worms take bass, but not as effectively as they take trout or bluegill.

To this day I'll swear lure manufacturers invented the largemouth bass. There are more artificial baits designed expressly for the catching of largemouths than any other baits. The reason for this? Bass hit artificials quite readily and, in the opinion of some anglers, a bass caught on an artificial is a better bass. The largemouth is an aggressive predator.

Top water plugs, jointed plugs, spinners, spoons, floating and sinking minnows, hair bugs, deep divers, leadheads, poppers, rubber and plastic worms—eels, crawfish, tadpoles—and sonic noise-producing lures have flooded the market. Every size, color combination and design can be found on tackle shelves. Some bass are just not at all finicky about what they attack. It seems the lures that flutter, wiggle, pop or sputter the most have bass catching promise. Some long-endured baits have proven their effectiveness.

Popping bugs are considered to be the most exciting and sporting way of catching bass. Fished on the surface with either conventional or fly fishing tackle, the popper has brought many a largemouth busting from the water. Resembling a large insect, frog, mouse or any other struggling tidbit, the popper is especially effective early in the morning or in the evening. It seems to work best when retrieved slowly with a series of pops and gurgles.

Rubber and plastic worms, eels or tadpoles that swim deep because of lead heads and equipped with a single (ordinarily weedless) hook, are probably the hottest bass catchers on the market today. Sometimes a single or double spinner of nickel or bronze is added to attract fish. Either way the bait has produced a special breed of bass fishermen. This, in turn, has produced special rods and special lines. The men who fish these rubber/synthetic baits are called "wormers." The rods they use are relatively stout. They are designed to "feel" the worm "crawling" its way along the bottom or over bass holding dens. They have enough backbone to set a solid hook into the thick-lipped old lunkers. Worm lines are limp monofiliment specialties designed and built not to stretch under the jaw hold of a stubborn bass. Some are designed in colors bright to the angler's eye, like yellow, but supposedly very hard to see by the bass. This feature enables the "wormer" to calculate the exact time when the bass has picked up the rubber bait and is mouthing it. When the line starts to move, the fish is running with it. Most wormers count to ten and then sock it to the fish. Worm line is not supposed to give or stretch under hook-setting stress, even at deep bass fishing depths.

Worming is an art that requires a good deal of patience. If not familiar with the technique, invite a pro to your pond. He will show you how. Worm colors alone are subjects of great debate among bass people. Purple is hot now. Black is good. But it would be safe to say that bass have been taken on every color of worm.

There are great varieties of artificial minnows mainly because the live version is the favorite food of the bass. Some are designed to float on top of the water until they are retrieved. When reeled in they shimmy just under the surface. These plugs are good for early morning and late afternoon fishing when the bass are working the shallows for baitfish. There are minnows designed with a metal lip in front which enables them to swim deep. These baits are especially effective when bass are feeding deep in midday. They are excellent trolling baits.

It is safe to assume that the current top bass lures effective in one area would be effective at ponds there, too. In time the fisherman will probably discover his own special bass killer. That's half the fun of largemouth fishing.

CATCHING BLUEGILL

The bluegill is the bread and butter fish of ponds and lakes in the United States. This scrappy sunfish can withstand heavy fishing pressure. And probably please more boys and girls than any other species of fish. The bluegill is considered one of the hardest fighting fishes for its size in the country.

Tackle

For bluegill tackle, think small. Ultra-light gear is sporting. Lightweight cane poles serve the purpose, too. The bluegill is not finicky. He's a crowd pleaser and he's fun to catch anytime. As a table treat, he compares with trout and bass. An angler just has to catch more of them for a meal.

Small hooks, small baits, small lures catch big bluegills. Kids and adults alike enjoy catching bluegill, with a float (cork or bobber) and hook baited with a garden worm. There's a lot of pleasure in watching that cork bounce up and down and finally disappear under the water. And then the zig-zag, underwater tussle that the fish puts up is as much fun to most anglers as landing a 100-pound sailfish.

Garden worms, grubs, catalpa worms, meal worms, crickets, small grasshoppers and katydids make good bait. Cast baits with a float or with little or no weight for a natural appearance. Leave some slack line when fishing without a float. When the line starts moving and tightens up, set the hook.

Small shiny lures, under an inch in length, catch bluegill. Tiny popping bugs with rubber legs are deadly when fished slowly with spinning or fly rod gear. Dry and wet flies are good. Imitation red and black ants are panfish favorites. And dry flies of every type will take sunfish when they are feeding on top. Woolyworms, bumblebees, imitation grubs and small jigs will also fool them.

Ice Fishing

Bass become extremely sluggish under the ice and in the winter are rarely caught by anglers. Bluegills, on the other hand, are voracious winter feeders. They are fun to catch and the more of them harvested the better the fishing will be. Cut a hole in the ice. Live baits mentioned already will work well. And so do tiny jigs, ice flies and lures. Fried golden brown in the skillet, a string of bluegills is a welcome wintertime treat.

CATCHING CHANNEL CATFISH

Only rarely are channel cats caught on artificial baits. But a number of natural and prepared baits are good for cats. Worms and nightcrawlers are standbys. Dead minnows and cut fish are good. Dough balls, blood baits, liver, entrails and other such delights attract catfish. Use hooks large enough for this fish's big mouth.

Tackle is a matter of choice. There is not much casting involved. Stillfishing predominates. Medium to heavy gear is recommended according to the size of fish. Evening and night fishing, during the summer months, are good times to catch channels.

Since the management of channel catfish ponds is not emphasized in this book, only brief comment about them is made here. Where channel cat fishing ponds are carefully managed,

(SCS)

Fish pond angling can be as simple or fancy as you want it. Here a family enjoys tussling with big fish.

good fishing results. As gamefish, though, trout, bass and blue-gill outrank the channel cat under farm pond conditions.

FACTS FROM A SURVEY

A national survey recently reported some interesting facts about fishing. It showed that 50 million Americans fished at least once that year. This represented 466 million man-days with 1.1 billion pounds of sport fish being caught. The single largest group of sportfishermen fall into the 45 to 65 age bracket. The second largest, the 35–45 group.

The United States population is expected to double by the year 2000, while anglers will increase about two and one-half times. This means that by the end of the century, about 63 million fishermen will be looking for a place to drop hook and line.

Wouldn't it be good to have your own private fish pond? Don't you wish everyone did?

9 | *Making Money*

FEE FISHING, FISH FARMING AND THE RAISING OF BAIT MINNOWS are important activities within the realm of the pond owner. But the commercial endeavors open to fish pond managers are not the primary reasons why this book was written. Instead, this book is devoted to the fish pond as a source of sport fishing, free and clear of the hard, cold business tactics of making money. Sport fishing ponds are designed to help anglers leave the worries of the business world behind.

Raising fish for profit does have a place in the overall picture of fishing pond operations. And for this reason, the pond owner should be aware of the various aspects of fish farming or fee fishing.

FEE FISHING

As a boy growing up in the suburbs of a large metropolitan area, fee fishing played an important role in my life. Not far from where my family lived in Prairie Village, Kansas, several fee ponds were within bicycling distance. For a modest fee ranging from $1.50 to $3.00, I could fish all day long and tote home a pretty good stringer of fish on the handlebars of my bike.

For the most part, the ponds I fished were stocked with bullheads (hard to manage, but easy to catch) and carp. Now I have already mentioned reasons why the private pond owner would be better off not stocking these species. But the fee pond operator is not so much concerned about stocking game-fish as he is in satisfying customers with quantities. The bullhead and carp provide quantity and fishing fun.

Fee-fishing ponds, fish-out ponds or put-and-take ponds have one thing in common. Catchables are usually stocked for instant fishing. This method of stocking provides immediate financial returns for the operator. Less emphasis is placed on total management than in planting the fee pond with reasonable-size fish that can be caught.

Warm water fee pond operators also stock their ponds with bass, bluegill, crappie and channel catfish. I fished several of these ponds throughout various parts of the Midwest. Unfortunately, I never found the fishing good at any of them. The average bass would run under a pound. Bluegills and crappie were ordinarily stunted around the four-inch mark. Some of the ponds did provide good fishing for channel cats. But, in general, the gamier the warm water fish, the poorer the fishing in fee ponds.

I believe there were several reasons for the poor fishing in these ponds. First, the bluegill and bass ponds I fished were free ponds open to the public. The scarcity of good state lakes and streams in the area made them extremely popular. Rather than drive 50 or 60 miles to reach public fishing for bluegill and bass, many anglers took advantage of the fee pond operator's advertisements offering good fishing.

The result? Heavy, heavy pressure. After a new planting

the fishing was hot. But give the bass and bluegills a few weeks to smarten up and fishing resembled that of a crowded public lake.

The problem of poor fishing goes deeper. In an effort to provide immediate financial return, most fee pond operators disregard rules of fish management. Catchables are stocked. These have a high mortality rate. Stocking, which should take place often in this type of fishing, is often put off until very few fish remain to be caught. In an effort to make a profit, some fish pond operators cut corners in stocking. This hurts a put-and-take fishery.

There are some fee ponds which are run very efficiently. For the most part, these ponds feature limited membership on a fee basis. The pressure can be regulated to insure good fishing for members. Sound pond management techniques are followed in most cases since the pond operator has the time to control the pond. Accordingly, he can meet his responsibilities to the pond, itself, the watershed and the fish contained in the pond.

Groups of anglers or sportsmen's clubs often lease the fishing rights to well managed fish ponds. The pond manager could be a farmer or rancher. Urban and suburban residents may also lease their ponds to fishing groups. Firm regulatory measures are needed in maintaining fee ponds that will be used by large numbers of anglers. The good fee ponds incorporate those measures. Poor fishing results from lack of control.

I place some ponds in the U-Ketchum category. This type of fee fishing seems most prevalent among cold water fee operators. Anglers catch trout and pay for each fish caught or by the number of total pounds caught. Trout pond operators do not have exclusive rights to this manner of fee fishing—some warm pond operators follow the some procedure.

There is one good point for U-Ketchum ponds although not all anglers would agree. Persons, mostly children, who have never caught trout and most likely would not have the chance again, do have an opportunity to do so at these ponds.

Some of the ponds themselves are scarcely bigger than bathtubs. Others resemble hatchery raceways or holding ponds. There is little, if any, esthetic virtue about the ponds. But trout catching is at least fast—and in some cases guaranteed.

Persons can catch as many fish as they want. Or a liberal limit is set at most ponds.

Some sportsmen do not consider catching a fish from a U-Ketchum pond a good experience for a child or person who has never caught a trout. They feel the experience is likely to be regarded lightly. Unlike the wary trout of well managed fish ponds located in natural surroundings, the U-Ketchum experience may be remembered and treasured in the mind of a young angler no more than would be a visit to the average fish market.

Again, there are exceptions to the rule. Some pay trout fishing resembles quality fishing. But the U-Ketchum pond operators seem to outnumber the serious pond managers.

The number of U-Ketchum ponds, both in areas where there are plenty of natural trout streams and in areas where only warm water species prevail, are due to the fact that put-and-take trout are relatively simple to maintain. The trout can be stocked as catchables, easily caught with worms or flies, and then re-stocked.

I remember the first time I was ever introduced to trout fishing. It was at the boat and sports show at the Kansas City Municipal Auditorium. One of the highlights of the show (and still is as far as I know) is a swimming pool-like pond filled with eight to twelve-inch rainbow trout. Fly rods, equipped with flies, are provided to customers paying for the right to fish for a specified time of, say, ten minutes or so. For hours, while my mom, dad and sister would look at the new boats, I watched great numbers of children and adults trying to catch trout. Even under such artificial conditions, most persons hooked at least one fish. Some of the old pros (the guys with their trout vests on) would catch maybe two or three. The fish were then cleaned and frozen. A customer picked up his or her catch before driving home that night. The pond was operated in conjunction with local Trout Unlimited Chapters in the area so the money was going to a good cause. I always wondered though about the manner in which persons unfamiliar with trout fishing were introduced to the sport. For some reason, I never tried my skill at the Auditorium pond.

The great number of U-Ketchum ponds in prime Rocky

Mountain fishing areas has always amazed me. For example, there is one such pond, apparently named U-Ketchum, near Afton, Wyoming. For those who have never been to Afton, let me say this. Some of the best natural trout fishing in the Rockies is to be had within ten miles of there. The Salt River, an excellent cutthroat fishery, runs within a couple miles of town. Numerous smaller streams with big deep holes surround the area. Beaver ponds are plentiful. And the Snake River runs 40 miles to the north.

No, the U-Ketchum pond operator has not been brain damaged by fishing fever. In fact, he has a desirable location for a fee trout pond. Nonresident and resident anglers both, defeated by wild trout, have a second chance at the U-Ketchum pond. After all who wants to go home skunked?

The characteristic of trout being able to adapt to any water cold enough to maintain them under artificial conditions, means they are ideal for all types of fee fishing.

Aside from the U-Ketchum ponds, there are some cold water ponds in which a fishing fee is charged per pole. Some ponds are situated in esthetically pleasing areas. Quality trout fishing can be enjoyed for a price. Many such ponds in the West are open for fishing on a membership basis. And, for the most part, good to excellent trout catching prevails. But the price of good fishing is sometimes high. One old gentleman I knew in Cheyenne, Wyoming, paid $350 per year to belong to such a fishing club near Laramie, Wyoming. For an 80-year-old man who couldn't wade wild streams as good as he used to, but still passionately loved fishing, the fee was probably worth it. The operators of the pond knew that elderly anglers make good customers.

RAISING BAIT MINNOWS

Despite the glittering array of artificial lures on display at sporting goods and discount stores throughout the United States, the demand for bait minnows is still great. Sometimes it's just more fun to thread a hook through a lively minnow, set a cork at the right depth and toss the offering to minnow-loving fish. Bass, pike, pickerel, walleye, perch and some species of trout consider the live minnow tops on their food list. When artificials don't tempt bass into hitting during midsummer doldrums, minnows fished deep often will. The minnow angler is a patient fisherman. He is willing to rest his body and soul on the bank of a peaceful stream while the baitfish on the hook does all the work. Some of the largest gamefish on record have been caught on minnows.

There is more to raising bait minnows than meets the eye. As with various species of gamefish, different species of bait minnows do better in some areas. Management techniques are of prime importance to the bait raiser. Since the complexities of baitfish management could take an entire book in itself, the best way to find out about the details is through the help of a local SCS technician. He can assist with design, construction of rearing tanks and ponds, and water management.

The individual considering going into live bait production— minnow sales in particular—well, he has my admiration. It's a tough business. And only the patient, strong willed man can make it. One bait dealer, especially, stands out in my mind.

For some reason, minnow sellers were scarce in my area of Kansas. But there were times during midsummer when the bass and crappie were particular. Four-inch shiners worked well on largemouths and two-inch minnows were deadly on crappie.

There were two companions with whom I fished regularly. Bernie Denk and his son Dan, ardent anglers, put me in contact with Al, minnow dealer. Our favorite fishing pond was about 20 miles from where we lived, but the bait dealer was six miles in the opposite direction. So, instead of getting up at five in the morning on Saturday fishing trips, we rose at 4:30 to allow for the time it took to go buy minnows and still get to the pond by sunrise.

Al's live bait shop was near an industrial section of Kansas City, Kansas . . . not where you'd expect to find a bait shop at all. We made the trip every Saturday—usually in the darkness of pre-dawn. A single, naked light bulb would be the only evidence of life in the fishy looking shop. One could hear the gurgle of the minnow tank aerators. On just the right mornings, there'd be the aroma of minnows that had perished during the night. Minnow mortality is rather high, even to professional bait dealers.

On a small but clearly printed black and white sign over the door bell were the words "RING FOR SERVICE . . . ANY-TIME DAY OR NIGHT." Somehow I would cringe at ringing the extra loud bell (more like a school alarm) that early in the morning, but one of us would do it and then step back quickly. There were times when we had to ring three or four times. But Al never failed us.

First the light in the hallway would signal his coming. Then some loud grumblings followed by a ring of cigarette smoke. Finally Al would appear. With bags under his half-closed eyes and a salt-and-pepper beard he was not a picture of joy when he opened the door.

"We need four dozen minnows, Al—break 'em up for bass and crappie and make them lively," Bernie would order.

In his methodical way, Al would scoop just the right number of minnows into our bucket. If the number was short, he would toss a few more into the can. If he got a few too many in the net he didn't bother to subtract. He was that kind of minnow salesman. And for his efforts we paid him one dollar per dozen for the large size and 75 cents a dozen for the for the smaller minnows. We'd say goodbye and goodnight to Al . . . thank him for being the only bait dealer with enough will power to stay open. And then head for the bass hole. Somehow my heart was always with Al when we watched him turn and trudge upstairs for a few more winks. I wondered how long it would be before the next fisherman would ring the bell.

Returning some years later to say hello to Al, I was both pleased and dismayed at the change. At the customary hour of 4 a.m. before a Saturday bass jaunt, I pulled up in front of his shop. A new big black and white sign announced, "NEW HOURS 6 A.M. TO 10 P.M. LET ME SLEEP IN PEACE . . . PLEASE?"

And so ended a fishing era. Al had given in. No more pre-dawn trips for minnows. But somehow the loss of an hour's fishing and a few minnows were worth the few hours of extra sleep—for Al.

There is one way to get around the poor business hours the minnow selling business demands. Bait raisers can, if they choose, act only as suppliers to bait sellers, thereby eliminating direct sale to the public. Let someone else sacrifice sleep. There is only one drawback to this method of operation and that is a decreased profit for profits of minnow sales are shared.

On the positive side of bait raising, there are those loyal souls who are deeply concerned about the fish catching success of countless millions of fishermen. Certainly they sacrifice beyond the call of duty and bass fishermen the country over are grateful for their devotion and service.

FISH FARMING

The third category of fish pond money making involves fish farming. This entails raising fish to a desirable size and weight for commercial sale to individuals, restaurants, mink ranchers or fish pond owners. The two main species of fish that have proven themselves adaptable to fish farming practices are trout and catfish—more specifically, rainbow trout and channel catfish. Both are considered fine table fare and good restaurants all over the country feature such taste tempting morsels as broiled trout or channel catfish fillets.

In areas where limited quantities of fresh fish are available, fish farming has good economic potential. States in the Midwest, for instance, have accepted fresh fish from farming operations with open arms.

The process of successful fish farming incorporates intensive fish management. And the importance of a fish farmer's harvest closely coincides with that of the tiller of the soil. Water quality control, spawning, hatching, feeding fish, harvesting and marketing the crop are involved.

A fish farmer can grow his crop in small or large ponds. A number of small ponds seem to be easier to manage than larger bodies of water. And fish crops can vary from small fish for stocking, pan-size fish for food or for recreational fishing, or large fish for brood stock. One or all types of farming can be undertaken by a single fish farmer.

Both retail and wholesale markets are available to the fish

farmer. The wholesale market requires large volumes of fish to supply cooperatives, processors, jobbers and other large volume outlets. Farmers usually sell fish at a lower price per pound to such markets, but their marketing costs are usually lower.

The retail market, on the other hand, is usually for small volume sales. There fish are sold live or dressed. Both costs and sale prices are usually higher for small lots.

In fish farming the operator who has studied his market area first and evaluated it according to its need for fresh fish can determine beforehand the probable success of such an operation. But some farmers have gone into the fish raising business only to find their market area inadequate and transportation costs too great for profit.

Other enterprises the fish farmer might consider are opportunities to contract for the production of fish or eggs for the state fish and game agency. Also, dressing and selling fish through a local processing plant. Marketing frozen fish to areas outside the local market, however, is tough. Chances are, larger, more commercial operations are already handling the fish needs of urban or suburban areas.

In matters of commercial fish farming, the United States Department of Agriculture and, more specifically, the SCS will

(SCS)

Commercial catfish farming operation—a number of small intensively managed ponds, the total area here covering some 50 acres.

help a potential fish farming enterprise. They may recommend a prospective fish raiser first visit state or federal fish hatcheries in the area to see what the operation entails.

It is important to contact the state game and fish agency as to the license requirements which usually prevail in all phases of commercial fish operations. In most states, licenses are needed to operate fee fishing ponds, bait raising and sales, and fish farming. The rules are designed to protect the state's fishery. Criteria for obtaining licenses and permits are based on proper stocking methods and suitable species of fish.

Although veering slightly from this book's main course, the opportunities for making money from fish ponds certainly cannot be overlooked.

10 | *Fish Pond Ecology and Conservation*

THE CONSTRUCTION OF A FISH POND AND ITS GOOD MANAGEMENT HELP carry out the goals of both ecology and conservation programs. Some examples of conservation techniques, as encouraged by all agencies involved in pond management, have been mentioned in previous chapters. In this chapter let's consider how these techniques directly relate to the fish pond and its surrounding area. The fish pond should not only benefit the angler. Its pleasures may also be enjoyed by wildlife photographers, bird watchers and many others who also appreciate nature and value ecological balance.

ECOLOGY—DEFINITION

There is nothing complicated about the term "ecology." Briefly, it means a branch of biology that deals with the mutual relations between organisms and their environment. So an ecolo-

117

gist is one who studies or observes these mutual relations. And, contrary to some popular usages of the word, an ecologist is not necessarily a man or woman radically possessed with trying to convert everything and everyone "back to nature." Hopefully, we are all ecologists, because it is in everyone's interest to observe and maintain good relations between organisms and their environment.

Living by standards of ecology means that man should not disturb any natural environment beyond the minimum necessary to accomplish some rational goal linked to human needs. By creating a fish pond, one may be restoring ecological balance to a given area or he may be designing a new and better environment for an area originally devoid of a sound one. Either way, the satisfaction from such a project is personally gratifying.

CONSERVATION—DEFINITION

The term conservation is not so easily defined. There are several explanations of the term. Some persons believe conservation means "to preserve", which is not quite correct. Conservation can mean using what we have available to us in a reasonable and wise manner. Today, conservation is closely associated with nature and the environment. But in reality conservation can apply to many phases of our lives. We can apply measures of conservation when using electricity, gas and water. We can apply conservation measures in our eating and drinking habits.

Conservation is the rational use of the environment to achieve the highest quality of living for mankind. That's one definition. But it needs explanation. Quality of living for mankind . . . just what is that? Crowded, unfit apartment houses, black pluming smoke stacks, polluted rivers and smog are part of today's living. Where they fail is in the quality department. Conservation seeks to maintain an environment that is healthy, diversified and esthetically appealing to humans. For us, possibly, the end result of such conservation objectives is a rich and varied life. Can we ask for any more?

A fish pond is a source of healthy recreation. Most of us will agree the pond and surrounding area, when managed according to sound soil and water guidelines, is esthetically pleasing. And the pond and its watershed is an area of wonderful diversification. A well planned, well managed combination of land and water can yield a wealth of wildlife variety.

ECOLOGY AND THE POND

A fish pond is an ecological magnet. Within the realm of the pond's water and land is to be found a complete, natural world. There the organisms, namely fish, tadpoles, frogs, aquatic insects, ducks, muskrats, beaver and all water-dependent life, relate every day to the water and soil environment that sustain them. Here is total life in miniature. When the pond is healthy and conservation measures practiced, a pleasing world results. When a pond deteriorates, so do the organisms that depend on it.

Pond ecology is interdependence of water, soil, fish and wildlife. All of which are affected by the elements of nature— rain, sun, season and temperature. A fish pond environment provides new habitat for birds, reptiles, furbearers, trees and shrubs.

One SCS biologist from Minnesota said that a pond creates an entirely new ecological community. The pond's purpose is to hold water and sustain fish, rather than let water run off the land. After managing a pond and understanding its dynamics, a pond owner has gained valuable insight into far greater en-

The fish pond area will attract many varieties of wildlife.

vironmental problems, such as land utilization and over-population. When persons become involved with fish pond management, they develop an understanding of the natural processes which occur in the environment. And when this is understood, they are better equipped to participate in decisions on a broader scale related to resource use and management.

For children and adults alike, the fish pond is an effective, first-hand ecological experience. As a teacher of life's basic principles, it cannot be surpassed.

CONSERVATION, ECOLOGY AND THE POND

The conservation practices utilized in fish pond management have a direct effect upon pond ecology. While pond ecology deals with the relations between fish and quality water, for instance, fish pond conservation makes good relations possible.

For example, in Missouri a study of 91 fish ponds showed that 90 species of birds and 10 species of mammals lived in the immediate vicinity. Cottontail rabbits lived in the immediate area of 85 percent of the ponds, doves at 65 percent, muskrats at 63 percent and bobwhite quail at 55 percent.

There was a reason for this fondness of wildlife for fish pond areas. The ponds were fenced to keep out stock. The immediate area was planted with grasses, legumes, shrubs and trees. This habitat provided water, food and homes for the wildlife. This relationship is called ecology. And the planting of cover and food, along with fencing are conservation practices that enabled the relationship to develop.

West of the Missouri River in South Dakota, a study showed that 40,000 manmade ponds containing about 100,000 acres of water harbored 141,000 ducks. Previously few ducks had used the area, but the ponds established a new population of waterfowl there.

Field borders between cropland and woodlands are often unproductive and badly eroded. They make good pond sites if there is an available water supply and provided the immediate watershed can be planted to prevent erosion. When planted to

Conservation measures applied to the area increase its beauty and value.

adapted shrubs, not only does this conservation practice hold soil and prevent siltation, but wildlife is attracted.

In the Southeast, bicolor lespedeza, a type of shrub or bush clover, does well near ponds. Used as fence borders, it provides food and cover for wildlife. Observations made by the SCS have proven that the seeds of this plant are high-quality food for bobwhite quail.

In the Midwest, similar areas of erosion are potential pond sites. With an available water supply, areas around the pond are seeded with grasses and legumes to protect formerly eroded areas. Such unmowed cover provides undisturbed nesting areas for ringneck pheasants in the spring.

Windbreaks of trees and shrubs are planted near ponds in the Great Plains and western states. They provide food and cover for many kinds of wildlife. And they are considered one of the best nesting places for mourning doves.

Hedges, including living fences of multiflora rose, are common to the Midwest and Northeast. As pond borders, they are pleasing to the eye. They also provide travel lanes for deer, furbearers, birds and small mammals.

The planting of trees, especially evergreens in areas of good grass cover, creates ideal habitat for cottontail rabbits as well as other forms of wildlife. The pond owner may even consider

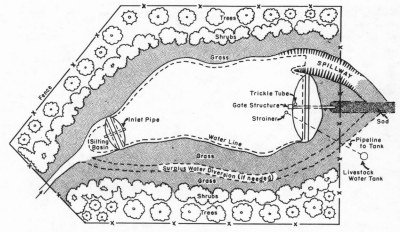

Landscaping is an important part of the overall conservation program.

planting some Christmas trees, along with permanent trees. While the Christmas trees provide good cover and hold the soil well, they can be harvested before they are large enough to shade out all the grass cover.

In conjunction with soil and water conservation of the immediate pond area, pasture improvement also benefits wildlife. The pond owner can suggest such practices to the rancher or farmer. The local SCS technician will then present conservation steps to improve the pasture. Fencing to control livestock use and tree planting may be the methods used. Where such practices have been put into effect, woodland wildlife such as whitetail deer, mule deer, wild turkey, blue and ruffed grouse have made strong comebacks.

In the western states, wildlife such as pronghorn antelope, and mule deer are fond of pond areas. When planted in grasses, woody plants and shrubs, the animals are drawn to the pond for water, food and cover.

Developing "odd areas" near ponds on farms and ranches is also beneficial to wildlife. These areas include fence corners, rocky spots, bare knobs, blowouts, sinkholes, borrow pits, abandoned roads and gullies. Planted with trees, shrubs and other plants that provide wildlife with food and cover, odd areas attract animals and birds, especially when fenced off from domestic livestock.

Aside from conservation practices already mentioned that relate to the pond and immediate area, watershed improvement is important. Patching eroded areas and preventing further erosion by planting banks and areas where runoff water flows are necessary. These guard against the number one polluter—siltation. Silt covers spawning beds, damages the gills of fish, and covers rocks, plants and gravel that support insect larvae and other fish foods.

Soil surveys help landowners make decisions regarding use of wetlands, near ponds. Marshes attract many forms of wildlife. Regulated grazing and planting to hold soil in such areas are ways to add to the wildlife wealth of the area.

In an earlier chapter, the restoration of strip-mine areas was mentioned briefly. In southeast Kansas, fish and game department experts have found that when strip-mine pits are filled with water and stocked with bass, bluegill or channel catfish, good fishing results. The surrounding area is planted in grass, shrubs and trees. What was once an area scarred to the point of being unusable has been turned into a valuable fishing resource. And when the areas are planted with wildlife-attracting food and cover, animals and birds of all types are drawn there.

(SCS)

This eroded spot has been turned into a place of beauty and good fishing.

Sometimes strip-mine land can be purchased by individuals or state conservation agencies. Either way, the land can be reclaimed and restored. Often times, the mining company that ravaged the land is willing to pay for part or all of the restoration process. And in more and more areas these days, companies that had gotten away with destroying land in the past, are now under public pressure to heal the land's wounds after they have exhausted its minerals and metals. Most companies are willing to pay the bill and restore the land to good use rather than risk a poor public image. To their credit, many have done this for years. With the help of the state conservation agency, the SCS and the Bureau of Sport Fisheries and Wildlife, thousands of arces of gutted lands are being nursed back to usefulness. And, they are being ponded and planted for good fishing.

Fish propogation in strip ponds has been good. Rarely do any shallow areas exist. And the water holding qualities of many mining areas make for good watertight basins. The result? Clear, deep ponds that support healthy fish populations. In fact, some of the clearest, deepest ponds in Kansas are reclaimed strip pits. Some of the best largemouth bass fishing is to be found in the strip pits of the southeastern part of the state.

Other states that are scarred from extensive strip mining can follow the lead of Kansas by turning such land over to the state or making it available for public sale, with the stipulation that ponds be built and the land be restored by conservation measures under the guidance of the SCS. Many pitted lands remain unclaimed and the project of its restoration given up as hopeless. But as land becomes more scarce, hopefully public demand will end the waste of valuable real estate.

Nearly every state representative, fisheries biologist or individual pond owner contacted in the preparation of this chapter stressed the importance of conservation in fish pond management.

In Missouri the most important goal of the state's conservation agency is the wise and prudent use of its natural resources for the protection and improvement of the environment. Fish pond construction and management is an important program in the overall concept.

In Minnesota biologists feel the role of the fish pond fits neatly into the concept of wise land use and, in turn, conforms to both conservation and ecological objectives.

Pennsylvania conservation officials say that the development and management of fishing ponds and the associated aquatic environment require time, effort and money. But more importantly in this day and time, it requires knowledge and understanding of the relationships between soil, water, vegetation and aquatic life.

In the building of fish ponds, Michigan biologists stress the use of irregular shapes in the water holding basins and their banks. In this way, they insure ponds that blend in with natural surroundings—so important to the total esthetic beauty of the area. The result of their efforts is a quality environment—part of the total conservation concept.

Iowa biologists stress the importance of pond construction to perpetuate the existence of aquatically adapted organisms.

Fish ponds in Vermont have added an ecological and esthetic dimension of beauty to the state's pastoral atmosphere. According to one SCS technician, "We have used creativity and imagination to fit ponds into natural settings."

Colorado biologists and pond owners feel they have added diversity to their environment. In a wonderful natural setting of trout streams and Alpine lakes, gentle, natural-looking ponds add variety to the showcase of water and surroundings.

In South Carolina, some fish ponds are planned and designed for Boy and Girl Scout camps. In areas where no ponds have been available to the Scouts, boys and girls are now able to learn current conservation methods and how they fit into today's concept of ecology.

In Arizona, the SCS has designed and built ponds for schools. Sometimes they are located in courtyards that were once only slabs of concrete. Now, when school children study conservation and ecology in school programs, they see first-hand the miniature world of life and how environment and organisms are dependent upon each other.

In the courtyard of the Lander, Wyoming, Junior High School, a pond sparkles in the mid-afternoon sun. Students on their way to classes admire it through large, panel glass win-

Even in the winter the pond is a resting and feeding area for these mallards.

dows. A pair of mallard ducks nest there. An occasional rainbow trout dimples the pond's surface in pursuit of a May fly.

There is little use of concrete, save for a narrow walkway around the courtyard. A healthy carpet of green grass waves in the mild Wyoming breeze. A cluster of aspens are planted in the middle of the yard. And near the aspens the grass and shrubs are not mowed. From the cluster of cover, the cackle of a rooster pheasant can be heard—the cock and hen break from hiding and scurry around the yard.

Within the courtyard's habitat are chukar and Hungarian partridge, too. Shrubs and plants of various types are living examples of the food and cover such wildlife needs for survival.

It would be much easier to maintain a courtyard of concrete but school officials and students of this school, under the direction of Conservation Center Director, Bob Legoski, have created a total environment outside the classroom windows. The idea, the effort, the view and the results of such a school project are refreshing.

Along with the pleasures derived from catching fat, spunky fish and full stringers, the fish pond manager inherits a complete, natural environment full of life. A new miniworld is created.

11 | *Pond Management*

THE POND OWNER WILLING TO MAKE A SINCERE, CONSISTENT EFFORT
at pond management will have good fishing and a rewarding
experience. It is as simple as that. But the pond owner who fails
to listen to the advice of experts or who tries to take short cuts
in management will probably wish the pond was never built.

It is the concensus of most SCS technicians and fisheries
experts contacted, that the main cause of pond failure is owner
neglect. Ordinarily the first two years in the pond's life and
the first year of fishing go reasonably well. Then some of the
glitter wears off. Like a new car that has lost its shine and
"new car" smell, wax jobs and tune-ups become less frequent.
We have a tendency to take things for granted after they have
been around for a while. Fish ponds are no exceptions. But
like the automobile, the owner who is conscientious about
maintenance will be rewarded by a lot of good fishing mileage.

Unlike the car owner, pond management is but a part of the total relationship. Maintenance is not drudgery, especially when it is performed on a regular basis.

One pond owner said his project has been a miserable experience. "The weeds are terrible and rough fish are always a problem," he said. "I would not recommend a pond to anyone." Somewhere along the line this man lost track of two very important management techniques—weed and rough fish control. Sure, they are problems, but they can be eliminated. Maybe this owner failed to heed the advice of his local SCS in pond construction. More likely, he did not have a complete understanding of fish ecology and management. Everything the owner does in or to his pond is interrelated.

Since a well managed pond yields several times the weight of fish than can be taken from the average pond, let's for the sake of discussion, divide the topic of management techniques into water quality and fish production.

FERTILIZATION

Fertilization is the process that raises the productivity of the pond's water. In fish growing, just as in crop farming, the more fertile the water, the faster the fish grow and the fatter they get.

Fertilizer provides nutrients for marine plants of microscopic size. This creates the bloom which colors the water with shades of green or brown. The bloom, however, shuts out the sunlight and discourages the growth of rooted underwater plants.

Fertilizer also increases the growth of fish food. The amount of food depends on the natural fertility of the pond's water. The pond is exceptional if it needs no added fertilizer because natural waters have low or moderate fertility and usually always need additional commercial fertilizer for good fish production. New ponds, therefore, should be fertilized as soon as they fill with water. And the fertilization process should be continued throughout the life of the pond according to the water's needs.

While fish, themselves, do not eat fertilizer nor do they, for the most part, eat the tiny plants or bloom, they do eat the worms, insect larvae and the like that feed on such tiny plants.

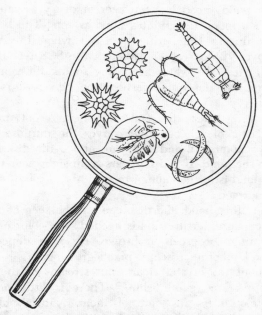

Fertilizer increases the number and growth of algae and aquatic food.

It takes about four or five pounds of aquatic animals (insects, worms) to produce a bluegill of one pound. And it takes four or five pounds of small sunfish to grow a one-pound bass. A high production of microscopic plants in fertile water therefore will result in more pounds of fish.

The time to fertilize varies according to different parts of the country. In Florida and southern sections of South Carolina, Georgia and the Gulf states, fertilization can take place year-round.

Farther north the growing season begins in early February and continues through late November. In North Carolina, Tennessee, Missouri, Arkansas and Oklahoma, it is usually warm enough in early March to start fertilizing and this can be continued until the cool weather of October or November.

The amount of fertilizer varies with each pond. Only after keeping fertilization records can the individual pond owner determine the amount and type of fertilizer best for the pond.

In general, ponds need less fertilizer in dry years and more in seasons when much rain dilutes pond waters. The best time to fertilize is during the spring and fall when the weather is cool, not over 72 degrees F. Although the SCS technicians may scientifically test the water according to alkalinity and acidity content, you can determine fertilization needs yourself with a simple device.

Nail a white disk to the end of a stick. A bottom cut from a white plastic bleach container serves the purpose. Mark the stick at two points, 12 and 18-inches above the disk. Submerge the disk in the pond. If it disappears from sight near the 12 inch mark, the pond is fertile enough to feed about 300 or 400 pounds of fish per surface acre.

If on the other hand, the disk can still be seen at a depth of 18 inches or more, fertilization is needed. The color of the water may be a tinge of green or brown. Its color depends on its number and kind of microscopic plants growing.

What about the crystal clear trout streams of the mountain areas that produce good fishing? There is little or no tinge of fertile cloudiness in some of them. Natural, clear water trout streams have built-in fertility. But in no way does their natural fertility match the created nutrients of a fish pond. In fact, some trout streams with gin-clear water have extremely low rates of fertility and their fish production and growth is poor. Some fisheries experts say that such water is low in nutrients. In these instances, stocking results are invariably poor.

There is one such stream in Wyoming called the Sweetwater. Legend has it that a miner back in the late 1800's was crossing the stream with his paniers loaded full of sugar for camp. The mule spooked midstream and the cargo was washed away— hence the name Sweetwater. The truth is that the water from this stream is actually sweet—rich in mineral content—but extremely low in nutrients. As a mild laxative, the stream water rates high, but the game and fish department rates it low as a productive trout stream. Although one or two stretches of the stream are heavily stocked and fishing is good there, the natural reproductivity of trout and their fast growth are virtually nil throughout most of the stream. Yet its waters are crystal clear.

There are clear trout and smallmouth bass streams that do

produce good fishing. Their fish growth and reproductivity are good. The streams, despite their clearness, are naturally rich in nutrients. Such waters are characterized by an abundance of aquatic insects and natural food. Tumbling riffles and deep pools are rich in oxygen. Some of man's fertilizer, such as limestone or ammonium sulfate, may be entering the stream through run-off or another water source. While too much accidental fertilizer could kill the fish, in small doses, the nutrients do help wild fish populations.

Some of the best trout streams in the country may be gin-clear in the fall during low water periods. But for the most part, the best fishing occurs when the water is somewhat cloudy in deep pools due to microscopic plant blooms. The necessity for fertile water conditions applies both to fish ponds and "wild" waters.

Fertile Bloom Versus Turbidity

There is an important difference between water tinged with fertile cloudiness and water that is turbid. Turbidity is that state of water where sediment is disturbed and suspended. In such case the cloudiness is due to the muddiness and it inhibits the production of fish foods. Turbid water can be a product of an inferior water-holding basin. Some soils will mix with water to produce turbidity, while others are easily made water-tight and have good clay-type adhesive qualities.

Of itself, the pond's water source can also cause turbidity. A strong flowing stream channeled directly into a pond, for instance, can cause roily water. The same thing may happen during periods of heavy rain. The stream draining a watershed might move with such force that it would not only produce turbidity within its own water, but affect the pond it flows into. This further illustrates the need for good water source controls. The ability to divert water so that its flow is controlled during heavy rain periods is important. This is why a heavy stream current should not be allowed to flow through the pond. Its flow must also be controlled to permit a constant water level. This adds oxygen and food to the pond water. Also the water flow must not be allowed to be too strong lest it nullify fertilization efforts by washing the nutrients out of the pond.

Recall that springs were mentioned as prime water sources. They cause a minimum of sediment disturbance and turbidity. And with such water source the pond is not affected by heavy runoffs.

Turbidity control, for the most part, can be eliminated through the choice of pond site and in the type of soil to be used for the basin. There are times though when some turbidity can result, even in the best planned ponds. Waters can stay muddy for even a year or longer after construction. The disturbance of certain soils, although they be quite adequate for a watertight basin, can cause very small soil particles to remain suspended in the water. But there are ways to control this type of turbidity.

Such a pond can be cleared by scattering 50 pounds of superphosphate and 100 pounds of cottonseed meal for each surface acre. If the pond is extra muddy, amounts can be doubled. Best time to do this is in the spring or fall; heavy applications of cottonseed meal might lead to an oxygen deficiency during hot summer months.

Another alternative is gypsum. Like other recommended mineral controls and fertilizers, gypsum used in prescribed amounts is not harmful to fish, livestock and humans. About 500 pounds per acre of gypsum can be scattered on the pond. The water usually clears in one or two weeks.

Another way to clear up muddiness is to scatter hay in the water along the edges of the pond. The hay draws the soil particles together like a sponge. (Hay is used, too, in controlling and soaking up oil slicks.) For each pond acre, seven to 10 bales of hay are adequate. The bales can be broken into blocks before scattering. If the water is not cleared after ten days, repeat the treatment. However, avoid using this method during periods of hot weather; deterioration of the hay could cause oxygen depletion. Scattering grass clippings on the pond surface also works.

Iron-free aluminum sulfate (alum) clears muddy water. Spread it over the pond's surface at the rate of 250 pounds per acre. Agricultural limestone does the job, too. Spread it on the water at a ratio of 1000 pounds per acre. These various ways are mentioned because methods of choice vary in different parts of the country.

FERTILIZING THE POND

A pond fertilization program can be set up by a SCS technician if the pond owner asks for such a plan. The benefits of fertilization have been mentioned. Weed control problems can be substantially reduced by fertilization. Pond nutrients are significantly increased. Now, one might ask, why doesn't the SCS consider fertilization fully as necessary to the pond as a trickle tube? There is, then, the other side of the coin—the reasons why fertilization is not heavily stressed. Biologists, by and large, feel a well planned, well managed system of fertilization is important to the fish pond's success in most parts of the country. These experts agree though, that fertilization should be approached with caution. Improper fertilization can result in excessive weeds or filamentous algae growth. It can also kill fish by oxygen depletion. In some respects fertilization can be likened to modern drug and antibiotic use. In prescribed dosages, applied by knowledgeable persons, such drugs prevent and cure diseases. Improper use of drugs can work the other way; instead of curing, frequent use or overdose can kill.

The same holds true when fertilizing with minerals. Improper usage can work in ways opposite those of proper usage. Think of pond fertilizer as a drug, just to illustrate. A vaccine that can add vitamins to your pond and prevent such diseases as aquatic weeds. And consider the application of such fertilizer from the standpoint of a doctor when prescribing and using drugs.

For understandable reasons, biologists who would otherwise recommend a program of fertilization have tended to play down this management technique. In too many cases, fertilization abuse, like drug abuse, has killed rather than helped. In most instances, where pond owners do not want to accept the responsibility of fertilization, only an initial fertilization after the pond is filled, is recommended. Even then sometimes only the use of agricultural limestone is suggested. This is a reasonable substitute for fertilization; it does increase pond productivity to a degree and without undesirable side effects. When comparing it to medical terms, however, limestone can be like aspirin—effective for colds, but not strong enough to prevent or correct major ailments.

What to Use

Mineral fertilizers are best suited to fish ponds. Organic ones such as cottonseed meal, blood meal, offal, manure and leaves encourage filamentous algae (sometimes called "pond scum").

A good fertilizer analysis is 8–8–2 or a ratio of 4:4:1. This simply means that each application provides eight pounds of nitrogen, eight pounds of phosphate and two pounds of potash per surface acre. At each application, use 100 pounds of 8–8–2 fertilizer per surface acre or a stronger mixture of fertilizer such as 16–16–4 quantities of 50 pounds per acre. There are variations to this formula, according to states, but in general this is good for both cold and warm ponds.

In the spring, you can fertilize from three to six times at 10-day intervals. The "white disk" test will show the best intervals. When the water shows signs of clearing add fertilizer to restore correct color. Color change should be apparent within three to seven days. Most ponds require about 12 fertilizer applications each year. Those with little fertility or no running water source may need as many as 16. Ponds that require only two or three applications are unusual.

Some pond owners are overly conscious of a clear water pond, feeling that clear water means good fishing. It is sometimes difficult to convince them that the water, green colored from fertilization, is not a menace to either fish or humans. The fertilized water does not bar swimming or other recreational activities, either.

How to Do It

Distribution of fertilizer is done from a platform, the latter placed about a foot below the pond's surface, near the edge.

If the pond level fluctuates, the platform can be suspended beneath floats. Or it can be attached to dock supports.

Sacks of fertilizer are placed on the platform and slit open. Waves and currents mix the fertilizer throughout the pond. One platform is sufficient for covering 15 acres of water surface.

If a platform is not used, fertilizer can be poured from a boat or distributed by hand from the bank. Other devices for holding fertilizer are old life rafts. The bottom of the raft is taken out, replaced with loosely fitting board supports and then covered with burlap. The sack of fertilizer is then emptied into the raft.

A wooden box attached to two oil drums works too. And an innertube covered with burlap is a reliable fertilizer spreading device. Chances are the pond owner will have one or more of the materials on hand for rigging a fertilizer distributor.

It is not necessary to scatter fertilizer all over the pond. And it is best to place it in water no deeper than three feet. An application along two sides of a pond is adequate.

Weeds—Good for Nothing

Waterweeds eat up the pond's fertility, interfere with fishing and provide no food for sport fish. A certain degree of misunderstanding seems to be associated with gamefish and cover. In larger lakes and streams, concentrating fishing efforts near weed beds or over brush seems to be the rule. And true,

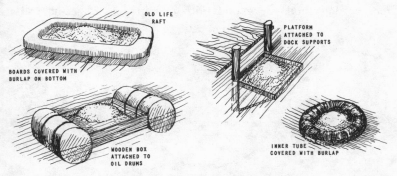

Illustrating various devices for spreading fertilizer over the pond.

some gamefish like bass, pike, pickerel and crappie do like shallow, weedy areas. But this is because minnow lovers like bass and pike frequent the shallows early and late in the day in pursuit of the baitfish that live there. At other times, they find cover in deeper water. Most anglers concentrate their fishing efforts in the morning and evening. Consequently, they fish the shallows. They catch fish there and hence associate shallow, weedy areas as the ingredients for good fishing.

One technological advancement that has put a hole in the "shallows theory" is the advent of electronic fish finders and depth recorders. Amazingly enough, anglers are finding fish in deep water, too, areas that seem devoid of any cover. And fish scientists are gathering proof that aside from prime early and late feeding times in shallow water, gamefish frequent the depths of lakes. Concentrations of fish are found in the deep water—away from weed beds, gravel bars and the usually known hot spots. New findings by fisheries biologists tend to prove that a fish's habits are related to available food and suitable water temperature. During midsummer a five-pound bass may prefer a lair at the 15-foot level far from the shoreline rather than in a shallow weed bed in the hot sun.

The quality of fishing to be found in a fish pond mostly free of weeds, snags and tangles also ventilates the theory that abundant cover means better fishing. I have always thought that a great variety of snags—weeds, trees, underwater brush and rocks—is more of a challenge to the angler than a factor directly influencing his catch. Some cover in the form of submerged logs and rocks undoubtedly can aid fish. But water

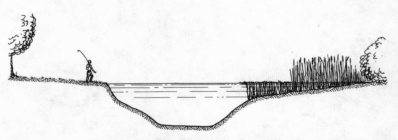

Shallow water means unwanted weeds.

depth is also a form of cover, and it is quite sufficient for the fish pond.

If some cover is nevertheless to be designed, especially in areas where summer temperatures runs high for protracted periods, try using docks, floating rafts or fertilizer dispensers. These provide shade and protection for fish. Baitfish will congregate there and in turn attract gamefish.

It was said that waterweeds are useless inhabitants of a pond. They may give an off-flavor to fish also. And when too many weeds die and decompose in the fall or under winter's ice cover, they create a low oxygen condition that could kill every fish in the pond.

Chemical and manual removal of weeds from a pond are only temporary measures. The best medicine is their prevention. Fertilization before weeds have gained a foothold offers the easiest method for their control. Weeds will return unless conditions in the water are made unfavorable for their growth. As mentioned already, this is best done by insuring deep edges during pond construction and keeping the water highly fertile. These two measures are the most effective and the least expensive ways for controlling most waterweeds.

Submerged weeds can be killed by applying fertilizer on their beds in winter. In Florida, December would be the best month. Farther north, January and Februrary would be the best times. This takes four or five months, but it is the safest and least expensive way to kill established weeds.

An 8–8–2 formula as mentioned earlier will work. Apply it by methods already discussed. Direct the fertilization over the weed beds, applying about 200 pounds for every surface acre. Repeat this every two weeks or until there is a heavy growth of single filament algae.

The procedure will totally shade the weeds and they will die in early summer. Thereupon they will float to the pond's surface, remain a few days and then sink to the bottom, there to quickly decompose. After their decomposition, the water turns from clear to green.

The reason weeds can be effectively eliminated by a winter fertilization program is that they are not growing at that time of year. An important requirement to winter fertilization, of course, is that little or no water flow through the pond. Too large a flow would counteract the effectiveness of fertilizer.

In the summer, a pond may have growing beds of submerged waterweeds. These would use the fertilizer and thrive to such proportions as to wipe out less hardy, microscopic plants and, in turn, rob the fish of needed aquatic food.

For temporary relief of weed problems, such emergent shore-line vegetation as cattails, sedges and rushes can be hand-pulled or raked out.

Although submerged vegatation is best handled by fertiliza-tion, it can also be controlled by shading using black polyethy-lene or vinyl plastic. This cuts off the sunlight. And mat-forming algae can be reduced by hand raking or dragging with a seine.

Floating weeds like duckweed can be controlled biologically by using 6 or 8 domestic ducks per surface acre. Ducks can control this weed, but it can also be prevented by clearing vegetation from around the pond so as to allow increased wind action.

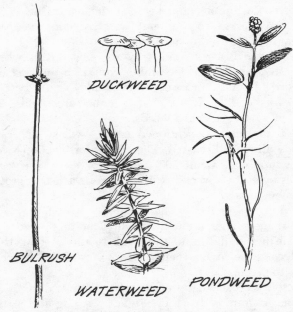

Various methods can be used to control pond weeds.

Weed control is temporary. The prospective pond owner can compare weed control to the problems of lawn care and controlling dandelions and crabgrass. Without chemical sprays, the weeding chores are quite frequent. Pond weed control is not quite as taxing, nor as frequent a chore, but there's some similarity.

Chemicals for waterweed and undesirable fish control should always be used with caution and at the advice of the SCS technician and game and fish department consultants. Permits must be obtained by the landowner from the Department of Health or the appropriate game and fish department before treating weeds or fish with herbicides or algaecides. The Federal Food and Drug Administration also restricts the application of chemicals in water containing fish intended for human consumption. Some chemicals fall under the heading of piscicides or fish controllers. Rotenone is one such piscicide in wide use by game and fish agencies today. The chemical affects gill breathing organisms and it is used to eliminate fish populations. It affects rough and gamefish alike, and its use is strictly controlled, even in state game and fish department projects.

According to Fred Eiserman, Fisheries Management Coordinator, Wyoming Game and Fish Department, fish killed with Rotenone can be eaten by man. Eiserman said, ". . . The amount (of Rotenone) that would have to be consumed would far exceed the amount that one could possibly expect to obtain from eating fish killed with the chemical." This was in response to a Kansas ruling, prohibiting the eating of fish killed with Rotenone, based on information which indicated that consumption of Rotenone can cause abortions in animals. And he added, "In fact, Rotenone has been used by South American Indians for taking fish for food purposes for many years without problems."

Similarly, Antimycin, a recently approved fish toxicant marketed under the trade name of Fintrol, is strictly controlled.

It is easy to understand why such controls are necessary on herbicides, algaecides and piscicides. Insufficient knowledge of control measures and abuse of such chemicals could seriously affect life and property. Extreme care must always be exercised to avoid contamination of public water, livestock or crops. Water sources, runoff or dam leakage make contamination possible.

The pond owner should be especially cautious of "quick and easy" methods to weed and to conduct rough fish control. There are none. And for that reason, draining the pond completely (as mentioned in an earlier chapter) by means of an outlet tube might be the best way to rid the pond of weeds and un-wanted fish.

Excess Acidity Harmful

Alkalinity and acidity can be controlled in a fish pond. This is called maintaining pH—simply a scale from zero to 14 that measures acidity-akalinity. From zero to six marks acidity; seven, neutrality; and eight to 14 denotes alkalinity. Trout do best when the scale reads 6.0 to 8.2 and warm water species thrive at readings of 6.5 to 9.0.

To raise alkalinity, the pond owner adds agricultural lime-stone in an amount specified by the SCS. Lowering a pond's acidity can be accomplished by scattering ammonium sulfate on the surface in amounts prescribed by a technician. Acid waters do not respond well to fertilization and ordinarily produce poor fishing. Excess acidity can be caused by soils deficient in calcium (lime). Sandy soils and sandstone areas may be par-tially deficient. In areas of known acidity, the SCS will probably recommend applying two tons of limestone per acre on the pond bottom before filling it.

Fish Need Air

Aeration, as concerned mainly with cold climates, is a form of manipulation that moves large volumes of cold, unoxygenated water from the pond bottom to the surface where oxygen can be replenished and toxic gases disbursed. In cold climates, aera-tion is an effective tool.

In areas where ice cover predominates the winter months, aeration keeps the water open. This can prevent winter kill—a loss of fish from lack of oxygen. The latter comes about when periods of prolonged ice cover kill plants by denying them sunlight. Then plant decomposition, especially in ponds without sufficient water space between bottom and lid of ice, consume the pond's oxygen. In the end this kills the fish.

Although mainly pertaining to cold climates, aeration can also replenish low midsummer oxygen supplies in warm-climate ponds. While this by no means constitutes getting to the root of the problem, during the height of the weed growing season, fish may be deprived of adequate oxygen levels and an aerator may prevent a die-off of all fish. Aeration, hence, is useful but it is only a temporary cure until adequate weed control measures are taken.

POND MANAGEMENT FOR FISH PRODUCTION

Feeding Fish

One form of fish management involves their artificial feeding. Little will be said about this since it is a technique designed mainly for commercial fish growing operations. It is reasonable to assume that when a satisfactory feeding program exists and good pond management practices are employed, fish poundage will increase. Private and state hatcheries feed pelleted food to promote growth.

For the pond owner whose main interest lies in sport fishing, a feeding program would make catching fish much easier for fish do reach a degree of tameness under regular feeding programs. However, where fish are made "suckers" for a hunk of liver or a piece of cheese about the same size and color of a food pellet, there is little satisfaction in fishing. But under intensely managed commercial fish pond conditions and for the raising of bait minnows, feeding is a necessity. Nevertheless, the only feeding I am concerned with is selecting the right lure or matching the hatch for that day's fishing.

Managing Fish

An important phase of pond management deals with the manipulation (by the pond owner) of fish populations. As already mentioned, harvesting all usable fish is important to balance, especially in warm water ponds. But in no manner can a pond, especially a warm water variety, be fished out. Therefore other controls or manipulations are needed to maintain balance.

In a warm water pond, the angler may have to put down the rod and reel periodically and harvest some fish with a minnow seine. Selectively removing 50 to 100 pounds of three to four-inch bluegills per acre each year helps fishing.

After several years, bluegills tend to overcrowd, even when under regular fishing pressure. Seining and trapping put an extra measure of control on them.

A fish trap constructed of one-inch wire-mesh chicken wire will do the job. Placed in four feet of water for at least two weeks during June, July or August, a good number of small fish will be caught. The trap could be baited, but that is not necessary. Once a small fish enters the trap, others will follow until the number snowballs. Remove the trap every other day and relocate it.

In a trout pond, harvesting by sport fishing methods is the most effective means of manipulating the population, for trout are not so easily caught in a minnow seine or by trapping. The highest annual yield of trout occurs when angling removes about one-half of the trout stocked the previous fall.

One of the primary causes of fish pond failure is the presence of one or several varieties of wild fish. Rough fish, catfish, crappie and perch have caused the downfall of some ponds. Keeping wild fish from entering the pond by means of grates or traps has been used with success. Stone filters built at inlets and outlets permit water to enter but prevent most wild fish from pond entry.

An overfall with at least a one foot drop where water exits the pond and returns to the water source, stops the upstream movement of wild fish.

One of the most common ways wild or unwanted fish enter a pond is through the good intentions of poorly informed anglers. Indiscriminate stocking causes imbalance. For example, an especially good largemouth pond I fished as a teen-ager was ruined in less than two years. A group of anglers were skunked there once; the next weekend they fished a public river and

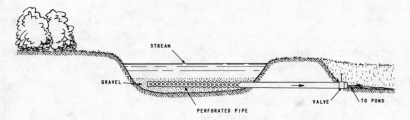

Gravel filters help keep wild fish out.

caught 83 bullheads. One of them had the bright idea to save all the bullheads for restocking purposes, so later that afternoon, they emptied the tubful of bullheads in the pond they had fished the week before. For the next two years the pond produced very few bass, but as many bullheads in the four-inch class as any angler would care to catch and no amount of seining could dent the bullhead population. To this day, I regret the loss of this once excellent bass pond.

Another way wild or unwanted fish may enter a pond is by permitting the use of minnows for bait. Sometimes rough fish minnows get off the hook or someone releases them in the pond after fishing. Bait minnows should be seined from the pond and fishermen should destroy them after fishing rather than releasing them in the pond.

Most of the more important pond management techniques have been discussed in earlier chapters. Correct pond construction, proper water temperature, adequate water supply and intelligent stocking practices all fit into the right management scheme. They fit together like spokes in a wheel. If any of them are neglected, the pond is adversely affected . . . weakened in some way. But together they virtually assure success.

Managing People

The topic of people management as a part of pond management has been saved for last. It is the toughest form of management for most of us.

It boils down to this: poachers, trespassers and uninvited guests should be discouraged from fishing the pond. One cannot always expect to be neighborly or friendly. At stake is the important problem of control. When one has planned, created and made good fishing, he will usually be willing to let those who have helped share in the harvest. But those merely trying to reap the benefits of the good fishing you created without permission can only hurt the pond. They are the same persons who may indiscriminately release unwanted fish.

Fencing, signs, locked gates and caretakers have been used effectively by pond owners. A fenced pond not only keeps livestock out, it lets the public know the pond is not intended for public use. Signs are vitally important. "No Trespassing" or "No Fishing" gets the point across in the briefest manner. If some fishing is to be allowed, a sign "No Fishing Without Written Permission" adds a measure of control. True enough, some signs may make the ordinary courteous sportsman angry. For example, on one large ranch near Cheyenne, Wyoming, the signs read "No Hunting, No Fishing, No Trespassing, No Fooling!" The addition of "No Fooling" raises the hackles of many an outdoorsman who would ordinarily respect private property. That particular ranch has had recurring problems of sign vandalism, fence destruction and trespassing—all due, I feel, to the matter of improper sign wording. The sign should be firm, yet polite; harsh words will not discourage trespassers.

At some ponds the access roads have locked gates. This keeps out the majority of the public, especially when a "No Fishing" sign is attached. In some instances a farmer or rancher may, at times, take on the responsibility of pond caretaker for a leaseholder. The farmer then decides who is allowed to fish and who isn't. For his services, he may be compensated with money or fishing rights. This is probably the most effective way of keeping intruders out.

Informing the SCS and local game and fish personnel that the pond is either closed or open to public fishing is also helpful. They can post interested sportsmen on the status of the pond ownership. The area game warden in his patrolling duties can keep occasional watch on the pond. There is no effective way of stopping poachers, however. Game and fish departments will vouch for that. Possibly the best measure is to avoid pub-licizing the fishing. But word of good fishing spreads fast and poachers have keen hearing.

Be firm but polite when dealing with anglers who ask permission to fish. A courteous "no" gets the job done more effectively than a harsh answer. One effective way of turning down fishing requests originated with a farmer in Missouri. He fibbed a little. But his reply got the job done in the fewest words possible. When he turned down fishing requests he would say the fishing in his pond was all reserved for his family, himself and the children from the local orphanage. Turned down anglers left with warmed hearts and smiles, not knowing there was no orphanage within 100 miles.

In dealing with trespassers and poachers, let the law handle the enforcement work. Be firm, but contact the authorities on problems. Do not try to take such matters in your own hands.

The other side of people management is to try to educate persons fishing the pond as to the rules set. These anglers may include members of the family, relatives and friends. Many times relatives take such excellent fishing for granted. But they, too, should be aware of correct stocking procedures, fish harvest policies and indiscriminate stocking problems.

Limiting the numbers that fish the pond can be a tough chore, "Say, Joe, you mind if I bring a friend next time?" are words familiar to the ears of pond owners. But unless you want to see all your planning, construction and management efforts go down the trickle tube, manage the pond closely. Better fishing will result for all concerned. And when help is needed in seining, stocking, fertilizing or draining, the persons who helped catch fish should be reliable volunteers.

Pond management is part of the fun of fishing. The owner's constant involvement will be accompanied by an ever grow-ing respect for the new fishing world created.

12 | *Trouble Shooting*

THIS CHAPTER DEALS WITH PROBABLE CAUSES AND SOLUTIONS TO various pond management questions and problems. Detailed explanations are omitted since most solutions—once pin-pointed —are treated in detail elsewhere in the book.

DISEASE AND PARASITES

Two topics, Fish Disease and Parasites, have not been discussed before inasmuch as rarely do fish diseases present significant problems in a well managed pond. They are sometimes encountered, however, in commercial hatchery operations or in minnow raising, where fish are handled frequently and live in somewhat crowded conditions.

There is no need to be overly concerned about fish disease and parasites. Chances are you will never experience a disease outbreak in your pond. If you do, check with local fisheries

146

experts on possible cures. Be aware of certain signs of diseased fish. But also realize there is no known successful treatment of virus fish diseases at present. The only practical controls are avoidance, isolation and sanitation. If the disease is diagnosed early enough, disinfection with chlorine and destruction of the infected fish may prevent disease spread. All infected fish should be immediately buried and pond equipment (nets, seine, fertilizer platforms) sterilized. Aquarium owners, who have had practical experiences with fish diseases before, know how fast a disease can spread in a fish population. This is why isolation and sanitation precautions have to be taken immediately.

Here are some signs of fish disease:

1. Sudden increase in fish mortality rate.
2. Fish swimming abnormally; this pattern may become convulsive.
3. Fish hanging vertically (instead of swimming).
4. Discoloration of fish.

Parasites—organisms that live off other living organisms—often become problems in crowded fish populations. Parasites are more common in fish farming operations, however, than in ponds used for sport fishing. But if adequate fish harvest is not obtained, parasites could gain control in sport fishing ponds also. Microscopic examination of a parasitic fish is necessary to determine a correct diagnosis. This examination is done by a fisheries expert. Internal parasites such as tapeworms and flukes are known to occur in many species of fish. The life cycles of the parasites and their exact effects upon a fish and its growth are unknown.

One known fact is that parasites affecting fish do not affect man. Any fish properly cooked and prepared is fit for human consumption even though it may have had parasites.

Treatments for parasites are only partially successful, even when found in early stages. The best control is prevention. Careful selection of fingerlings, too, is important. Make sure they come from disease-free sources.

Wild fish are carriers of some diseases and parasites. Prevent them from entering your pond by methods already mentioned.

Fish culturists from various parts of the country are not in agreement concerning the best treatment for fish diseases and parasites. Several possible treatments may be suggested by local fisheries technicians. Usually they will prescribe treatment according to water quality, temperature, the species of fish and the physical condition of those infected.

Since fish suspected of disease or parasites must be carefully examined it is necessary to trap or seine fish samples. The pond may have to be partially drained to do this, but by having fresh samples available, problems can be diagnosed sooner.

A handy booklet for warm water pond owners, entitled *Parasites and Disease of Warm Water Fishes,* is available from the U.S. Fish and Wildlife Service (see Bibliography).

TROUBLE SHOOTING FISH PROBLEMS

Problem	Probable Causes	Solutions
Fish Die-off	Low dissolved oxygen levels due to improper pond design; poor water source; improper stocking; poor management practices.	Aeration; weed control; harvest; eliminate existing fish population and restock. (See Chapters 7, 8, and 11)
Fish Die-off	Unsuitable water temperature for fish species planted.	Make water warmer—aeration keeps water circulating—cold water from bottom to top. Depth should be adequate for fish to reach cooler water. The addition of a colder or warmer water source. (See Chapters 1, 11)
Fish Die-off	Toxic pollutants.	Investigate water sources and watershed to pond. Runoff could be washing pollutants into pond. Be careful with insecticides and pesticides used near pond. (See Chapters 3, 11)

TROUBLE SHOOTING FISH PROBLEMS (*Continued*)

Problem	*Probable Causes*	*Solutions*
Fish Die-off	Parasites and disease.	Take samples and have them diagnosed by fish biologist.
Winter Kill	Lack of oxygen under ice cover.	Aeration and weed control before ice cover. (See Chapter 11)
Summer Kill	Oxygen depletion due to stretches of cloudy days with no wind. Prevents photosynthesis. High temperature with too much decaying matter.	Weed control is fundamental prevention. Seine-raking of weeds is temporary measure along with aeration. Scatter 50 to 100 pounds* of superphosphate when fish are showing signs of stress. (See Chapter 11) * See note, end of chapter.
Oxygen Deficiencies (not necessarily die-offs) Fish near the surface	Too many weeds; prolonged cloud cover, high temperatures.	Pump water from pond and spray it into the air to pick up as much oxygen as possible. Apply superphosphate at rate of 75 to 100 pounds per acre* to stimulate photosynthetic activity of aquatic plants causing them to produce more oxygen. Broadcast potassium permanganate five to eight pounds per acre foot* to alleviate oxygen shortages. In case of supplemental feeding—stop feeding altogether. (Ways to Prevent Oxygen Deficiencies, see Chapter 11.) * See note, end of chapter.
Stunted Fish	Overpopulation.	Remove stunted species by seining, trapping, fishing. Chemical poisoning may be recommended or pond drainage. (See Chapters 3, 8, and 11)

* "Acre Foot" is an SCS engineering term, not the same as "surface acre foot."

TROUBLE SHOOTING FISH PROBLEMS (*Continued*)

Problem	*Probable Causes*	*Solutions*
Fish Shock	Drastic change in water temperature—from one water to the other. Rough handling.	Mix receiving pond water with water in transport container slowly, until temperatures are nearly the same. Release fish gently. (See Chapter 7)
Poor Fishing	Poor fishermen. Too many weeds, oxygen deficiency. Over-population. Water temperature, water quality extremes.	Follow good fishing techniques. Best fishing times early morning and late afternoon. Proper stocking and fish pond management will produce good fishing. (See Chapters 7, 8, 11)
Disappearance of Fish	Introduction of highly predacious species; unsuccessful stocking; escape through faulty dam or outlet; disease; poaching; dam leak or break; inadequate spillway.	Prohibit promiscuous stocking and prevent wild fish; check stocking success periodically with seine or traps; follow suggested dam and pond construction methods; check fish behavior; fence and gate pond area and build spillway to handle heavy rainfall. (See Chapters 3, 7, 11)
Undesirable Fish	Inadequate control at inlet and oulet; indiscriminate stocking.	Grates and stone filters built to prevent upstream or downstream fish from entering pond. Educate persons using pond about fish management. Discourage fishing with minnows not seined from the pond. Follow stocking advice from SCS and game and fish department. (See Chapters 3, 7, 11)
Poor Fish Flavor	High temperatures; usually late summer; dense algae blooms. Fish take on flavor of vegetation, whether growing or decaying. Agricultural chemicals in spray form may drift over pond and cause	Reduce algae bloom by treating pond with copper sulfate at advice of SCS. Proper weed control discourages decay of organic matter. Keep livestock fenced out. Check streams or water source

TROUBLE SHOOTING FISH PROBLEMS (*Continued*)

Problem	Probable Causes	Solutions
	off-flavor. Oil spillage from water source. Livestock.	for leaks in oil pipe. Spray chemicals on windless days. (See Chapter 11)

TROUBLE SHOOTING POND PROBLEMS

Problem	Probable Causes	Solutions
Leaking Dam	Muskrat or beaver damage; poor soil and construction methods; inadequate trickle tube (not keeping water at proper level even in periods of heavy rainfall). Blockage of spillway; clogged grate.	Complete or partial drainage of pond to repair leak. Prevent situation by building on recommended soil. Follow trickle tube design installation as recommended by SCS. Do not grate nor filter spillway. Control beavers and muskrats by trapping. (See Chapter 3)
Pond Losing Water; not being able to maintain desired water level.	Prevention: Pond basin sealed watertight to hold water; unreliable water source—not adding	Drain pond completely and seal bottom and sides with bentonite. Channel a reliable water source

(SCS)

Fence keeps livestock away from pond, helps maintain quality fishing water.

TROUBLE SHOOTING POND PROBLEMS (*Continued*)

Problem	Probable Causes	Solutions
	enough water to make up for evaporation. Inadequate trickle tube.	into the pond. Check trickle tube for clogging. Make sure tube is of sufficient diameter during construction design phase. (See Chapters 3, 11)
Beaver Damage (In limited number, beavers add a valuable wildlife resource to the pond. In many ways they are fine examples of good pond managers, themselves. When controlled, they are a pleasure to have around and fun to observe.)	Beavers—especially significant in areas of heavy beaver concentration. They block water sources and bore holes in inadequate dams. On occasion they foul inlet and outlet tubes. Can cause muddy water.	In most states beavers are strictly controlled. Harvested in a limited number by licensed trappers. If a beaver problem, call local game warden. He will advise as to possible trapping methods. Preventing beaver destruction is better than continually unclogging drains and patching the dam.
Muskrat Damage (When the population of muskrats is controlled or harvested, these furbearers are also enjoyable to have around and a pleasure to watch and photograph.)	Muskrats dig into banks and along shorelines, removing and loosening soil. Sometimes they burrow into dams. They are not likely to cause serious damage if the dam is properly built.	Muskrats are not so closely controlled as beavers in most states. Game and fish personnel may recommend trapping muskrats with steel traps if they get out of hand. The fur of the animal is prime.
Crayfish (A limited number of crayfish, crawdads add good variation to a bass's diet.)	The main objection to too many crayfish is they can cause muddy water. They dig near banks and root in the mud along the shoreline.	Under the direction of SCS and only if there is a definite crayfish problem should they be controlled. A solution of four ounces of chloride of lime dissolved in three quarts of water will work when applied inside a crayfish burrow. Or a lye solution of eight rounded teaspoonfuls of lye in a gallon of water works. One cupful to a burrow.
Muddy Water (Not to be confused with cloudiness of fertile water.)	Pond newly constructed; suspended sediment. Beaver, muskrat or crayfish activity. Muddy water	Patience—in most cases new ponds will clear within a year. Muddiness can be cleared by various

TROUBLE SHOOTING POND PROBLEMS (*Continued*)

Problem	*Probable Causes*	*Solutions*
	source. Erosion due to lack of sod on dam and banks. Erosion of watershed; heavy rainfall.	techniques. Follow soil conservation practices to prevent erosion. Grass, shrubs and trees hold soil together. Heavy rains will tend to stir muddy water. This is natural and will disappear in two or three days. (See Chapters 3, 10, 11)

POND AREA TROUBLE SHOOTING

Problem	*Probable Causes*	*Solutions*
Snakes (Some water and land snakes should be expected. They are part of nature and help reduce insect pests and some rodents. Poisonous ones should be eliminated.)	Area around pond not cleared. An abundance of rocks, stumps or brush. High grass, unmowed. Too many weeds around pond.	Keep the grass cropped short. Clear area around pond of unnecessary stumps, dead fall and brush. Keep water weeds along bank down. Net or trap snakes—and if number grows too large kill them. Chances are that if area is well groomed, snake problem will be nullified. If poisonous varieties are common to the area, be able to identify them and eliminate them. Use extreme caution when trapping poisonous snakes. Use a long forked stick to trap snake. Use a long club to crush the head. Make sure snake is dead. Bury head and body, to avoid accidental scratching by fangs.
Insects and Bugs (Including chiggers, mosquitos, black flies, deer flies, and stinging insects.)	Part of nature that can rarely be fully controlled. They are especially attracted to shallow weedy areas of pond and to areas of high grass and weeds around pond. Some stinging insects nest in rotted downfall. Trash or garbage attract bugs; fish guts and fish	Keep grass mowed and clear pond area of unnecessary downfall. Avoid shallow weedy areas of pond in construction phase of pond. Do not let garbage sit. Pack trash in and out or bury it in suitable spot. Compost pile might serve pond owner well. It does not

POND AREA TROUBLE SHOOTING (*Continued*)

Problem	*Probable Causes*	*Solutions*
	scales and discarded fish attract them.	attract bugs, but is magnet for worms and grubs —top fishing bait. Bury, compost or carry out discarded fish and entrails. Use a fish cleaning board that can be washed.
		Some walking and flying insects will stay anyway. A good smoke fire keeps them away as do some better repellents. The long-lasting bite of chiggers may be avoided by not sitting on grass and keeping grass mowed short. Sulphur powder applied to all areas where clothing is tight will work if applied before fishing trip.
Frogs (Mainly feed on insects but adults are capable of eating small fish. Generally frogs are not problems, but excessive numbers should be controlled.)	Shallow weedy areas, unmowed, marshy banks.	Adult frogs mean good sport. Gigging or hand catching frogs is fun and frogs' legs are a delight on the table. This is usually adequate control.

Note

The quantities of fertilizer and chemicals for use as suggested under the *Solutions* column may vary with the size of the particular pond, the scope of the problem, etc. Double check with area SCS technician.

13 | *What Pond Owners Say*

THE PERSONAL POND EXPERIENCES OF OTHERS SHOULD BE OF CON-
siderable interest to all prospective pond owners. I was in
contact with many of them while preparing this book.

As a pond owner, myself, with numerous experiences with
planning, construction, stocking, fishing and managing ponds,
perhaps I am somewhat prejudiced in my thinking. Excellent
fishing has been my reward. But in contacting other pond
owners by personal visits, letters and telephone, I discovered
all their experiences were not necessarily good ones.

It is a pleasure to report, however, that the majority of
those who built and managed their ponds for sport fishing
were happy with the results. Those who built and managed their
ponds as commercial enterprises, on the other hand, were—in
more cases than not—disappointed with their experience.

In talking with the various owners, I was as glad to get information on the commercial pond operations as to learn what I could from those who, like myself, developed a pond purely for sport fishing. Experience in both types of operations, I thought, would confirm the importance of the management techniques stressed in Chapter 11. And, as contacts were made and evaluated, the remarks of persons currently managing fish or commercial ponds tended to support this.

UTAH

Steve Molner of Neola, Utah had some definite comments on fish ponding and his advice is certainly worth mentioning here. The questions in this first example indicate generally the ground covered.

Q. 1. Why did you build a fish pond?

"First, because I like to fish. I am an ardent fly fisherman and fish the pond with flies only. And we like fresh fish on the menu. All ten of us in the family like to fish real well."

Q. 2. How did you build it? Could you give me a cost estimate?

"I built the pond with the help of the Soil Conservation Service Office. And the total cost was about $2,500."

Q. 3. When did you build your pond and for what primary use? Who helped you with it?

"I built the pond in June of 1967 primarily for fishing. I also do some irrigating from the pond with a pump that brings water to my garden and shrubs."

Q. 4. What are some of the main problems of pond ownership?

"Too many people want to fish the pond and get away with it without asking permission. And when too many of the neighbors fish it, some accidents can result."

Q. 5. What are the rewards of pond ownership?

"To be able to fish when you want to. And I have learned the habits of fish. I really like to study them."

Q. 6. What advice would you give a person thinking about building a fish pond?

"Make sure you have the right materials for building the basin and dam. Fill material is very important and not all material makes good fill for dams."

Q. 7. Any data, not covered by the questions, which you believe would be helpful to the potential pond owner?

"My pond was built with a Cat and Dozer. But I ended up not having enough good fill material to cover all the basin and dam. My pond now leaks."

Mr. Molner reemphasized the importance of the general construction guidelines mentioned in Chapter 3. His dam leaks because of poor fill. This problem could possibly have been avoided when the pond was built. He is a good fish manager, being able to harvest enough fish with a fly rod to serve a family of ten. Possibly he needs to have stricter pond rules to minimize or eliminate the neighbor and poacher problems.

CALIFORNIA

Jack H. DeBoer of Waterford, California built his pond to raise fish and make a profit. From 1960 to 1973, he constructed 25 commercial ponds for raising fish. What are the problems of commercial pond management? According to DeBoer, the cost of such operations is a problem. He named parasites, fish diseases, weather, feed and water as expensive elements to deal with in commercial fish raising.

The rewards of the commercial fish grower differ from those of the man who builds a pond to catch fish. "Self-satisfaction when the operation is a success—profits are my rewards," said Mr. DeBoer.

James Kielhack from Austin, Nevada built his pond for fishing and swimming. "I enjoy having trout any time I want them and I'm interested in the fish, themselves—they are fun to study and observe," added Kielhack.

"I used a Cat (D–6) to dig out from the middle of the pond

and then a scraper to level the banks. I wanted the water level to be ground level without a bank. A rough guess of the cost, including labor and diesel but not counting my own equipment, would be around $1500."

Kielhack was aided by an SCS technician and SCS-related pamphlets in the planning and construction of his pond. The pond is six years old.

"There are problems tied to pond ownership," Kielhack stated. "A fish pond attracts a lot of 'friends.' It is necessary to come up with some sensible rules as to who uses the pond and when. An adequate supply of water is necessary—evaporation losses are quite high in the summer. And keeping the pond area clean takes a little time."

The rewards of pond ownership according to this angler are many. Kielhack said he takes great pleasure in watching persons who have never fished before get hooked on fishing. In giving advice to prospective pond owners he suggests to avoid building a pond that has any area shallower than three feet. Shallow areas grow weeds, the fish do not use them. And this was one mistake he made. "Otherwise, I am most pleased having a fish pond," Kielhack concluded.

OREGON

Sidney J. Nicholson, Florence, Oregon built his pond as part of a commercial venture. The pond is used to rear the trout raised in his hatchery. He constructed the pond for about $600. A drag line dug the pond alongside a creek so that its water could be diverted and used as a regular water source.

Nicholson raises some problems based on his dealings with fish ponds. "High water will wipe you out unless you can let it go by," he said. He also mentioned the problem of natural predators such as disease and phantom bass—those fish that attain large size and eat smaller fish. "Human thieves who will steal fish when they won't steal anything else are also problems," added Nicholson.

This commercial operator said he's never found any substantial rewards in pond ownership. And he advises would-be pond owners not to tackle commercial endeavors. "But if you do," he adds, "be absolutely sure the pond is engineered so you can drain it completely. That way you can work with the fish."

He further explained that fish raising on a commercial basis in his rural area is a losing proposition. But there are probably some areas where it is better. "A small pond for fun under good water conditions is a pleasure. But my experience was a financial disaster," Nicholson concluded.

MICHIGAN

Joel R. Young of East Lansing, Michigan built a pond in April, 1969 for the self-satisfaction of providing a resource for fish, fur-bearing animals and waterfowl. He wanted a recreational source for himself, his family and friends, too.

He used a crane with a 50-foot boom and a 1½-yard bucket to build the pond. Labor and construction cost about $1000. The SCS and the Michigan State Department of Fisheries helped him.

"Encroachment of poachers," says Young, is his major problem. "The rewards are many," he adds. "My family and friends now have a recreational area where they can fish and observe wildlife."

Young advises prospective pond owners to be sure and contact their local fisheries biologist when dealing with fish. And it is advisable to obtain design specifications on pond construction from the SCS.

"Be sure of a constant, clean supply of water, such as underground springs or a watershed of adequate size and having protective vegetative cover," Young added.

ARKANSAS

A. J. Troxell of Greenbriar, Arkansas built a fish pond for family recreation. He and his family wanted good fishing. They also wanted water for wildlife.

The cost of the pond was approximately $460. A cost-sharing program under the direction of the Agricultural Stabilization and Conservation Service helped finance the pond. The dam was

Trees, fences and shrubs will enhance the beauty of this area.

constructed with a bulldozer in 1960 and has proven a good water holding structure ever since.

Troxell had some problems, though. Runoff erosion affected his pond drainage area. He suggests a drainage area that is well-sodded. Trees help to hold the soil, too. This pond owner also emphasized the importance of controlling the number of anglers using the pond.

The rewards of pond ownership for A. J. Troxell (both he and his wife are retired) are many. "My wife likes to fish," Troxell said, "and our three sons and their families enjoy fishing when they visit us."

His advice to the prospective pond owner: select a silty clay soil with a well-sodded drainage area. This area should be about ten acres. Plan good spillways, especially in heavy rain country.

Troxell adds, "Our average rainfall is 48 inches a year. We fertilize to produce algae, which in turn feeds the bream and bass. Fertilizer is applied in March, April and May as needed. The quality of our water is so good the pond never gets muddy, even after heavy rains."

VERMONT

Another pond owner, from Vermont who wished to remain anonymous, created good fishing, boating and promoted wildlife conservation with a pond constructed in 1968–69. The U.S. District Agricultural agent (SCS), the Bureau of Sport Fisheries and Wildlife and the Vermont Resources Commission assisted her in its planting, construction and stocking.

"Actually," said this lady pond owner, "I reconditioned or revived an old pond by building a new, earthen dam. It made the fishing and quality of water much better than the original pond."

"There are so many rewards!" she continued. "I've stocked with rainbow and (speckled) brook trout. The fishing is terrific. The pond attracts and nourishes small and large game. I have a great variety of birds—wild geese, many ducks (which breed here), song birds, wading birds and cranes. We enjoy boating, swimming, picnics and the pond's peace and beauty."

The biggest problems according to the Vermont pond owner is supervision. Poachers, unauthorized children, and snowmobilers in winter present problems. "I keep a full-time caretaker at the pond and post conspicuously," she added.

Her advice: "In a new pond, great patience must be exercised. Undesirable grasses and weeds take time to die. Do not let anyone put herbicides of any kind in the pond. This will kill the small, unseen pond population, thus upsetting the natural balance."

"I encourage planning and building a pond as a source of lasting enjoyment," she concluded.

Numerous other contacts with pond owners ran much the same. Pond owners who designed their ponds of manageable size and with sport fishing as a prime purpose, were rewarded with good fishing and good experiences. But those who had neglected one or more of the SCS or fisheries biologist's recommendations supported, in their testimony, that there were no shortcuts to good fishing. The most common problems cited dealt with water conditions, weed control and fish life. Undesirable fish species was also mentioned by way of added problems. And pond owners with the most complaints had several things in common. They agreed there were few if any rewards in pond ownership. From their experiences they could not advise pond ownership to others.

My own experiences have been rather similar to those of the positive ones encountered. This is not to say that I enjoyed trouble-free pond planning, construction, stocking and management. I did not! But, with the help of the local SCS and fisheries biologist, I was able to anticipate and prepare for most of the problems even before the pond was constructed.

Not mentioned by other pond owners I contacted, one of my major obstacles was impatience. That is, as concerned the time from planning to the time when I could fish the pond for the first time. At first, the two-year wait seemed like too long, and several times I questioned whether the time, money and the wait was worth the effort.

But as it turned out, the true worth of our fish pond became quite evident shortly after it was stocked. Although I could not fish the pond, I thought of the water much as a farmer does when the green shoots of his seedlings finally appear above the ground. There is a good feeling of accomplishment within only a few weeks following stocking. Great satisfaction comes from knowing the planted seedlings or fingerling fish are growing.

I determined to make even the very first years of my pond's life enjoyable. Observing young fish and their habits, I discovered, was fun. I watched six-inch bass pop the surface for wind-blown grasshoppers. Occasionally, I tossed a worm or two into the water and watched four-inch bluegills race for first chance at the offering.

And once, sometimes twice a month, I would run a small minnow seine, with the help of a friend, along the four-foot depths of the pond. This was almost as exciting as fishing with hook and line, but I rarely handled the fish with my hands, unless one became stuck in the net. The main concern was to check size and general condition of the bass and bluegill. It was intriguing, after seeing the bass and bluegill fingerlings planted as rather colorless, undistinguishable organisms, to discover how the fish had matured. The bass were taking on a silvery hue and broad horizontal bars, running the length of their bodies, were readily distinguishable.

The bluegills, too, were bursting with color. From seemingly delicate fingerlings, they were growing into powerfully built, slab-sided sunfish. When they fought the grips of the soft cotton-mesh net, I could imagine how they would fight the willowy action of my ultra-light fly outfit.

I kept records on the fish using notebook charts divided into various categories. At the advice of a biologist friend, I headed its columns Approximate Size, Weight, General Condition, Visible Signs of External Parasites, Date, Pond Location and Time of Day. For a person mainly interested in catching fish on a rod, this perhaps was more potential bookkeeping than necessary, but it helped me to better understand and appreciate fish life and ecology. I became increasingly concerned about the fish and felt a closeness to the pond and its fascinating life.

Keeping close tabs on the development of bass and bluegill in the pond was a good sport in itself. At the same time, I was performing a management function that could help detect any problems developing in the pond before it was too late.

I'll never forget the time I found two eight-inch bass dead along the south bank one day. Floating belly up, the fish were near the stream source that entered the pond. I scooped them up with a net and examined them, feeling I had lost two bass that would have later proved good contestants on rod and reel. But part of the bass were chewed; one of the tails had been bitten off. In the soft ground at my feet were raccoon tracks near the bank. I didn't mind such a furry bandit catching a meal from the pond for until that time there had been no evidence at all of raccoons using the area. Evidently these bass had been working the shallows for insects, unaware of the hungry predator above on the bank.

When I finally fished the pond I knew just how large most of the bass and bluegill were. Also, that several fish had grown bigger than the others. They were extremely aggressive feeders and grew rapidly. I caught three of the larger-than-normal bass the first morning. And by the way, landing these fish was just as much, if not more fun than catching them from a wild stream. Having watched them grow from fingerlings up made the sport even better.

PEOPLE PROBLEMS

Over my years of pond management, I encountered only one main problem. I could not turn anglers away. Fishermen who asked permission to try their luck at our pond were usually given the go-ahead. I found I could not turn down another angler. Perhaps this is why the strong emphasis on fisherman control in pond management.

The number of anglers I invited and granted fishing permission snowballed. It wasn't until one May morning two years after the initial stocking and only a year since I had started fishing the pond that I was treated to a rude awakening.

When I arrived at the pond at eight that morning, six anglers already lined the bank. I knew only one of them! "How's the fishing?" I asked. The one fellow who had originally been granted permission to fish looked up somewhat sheepishly. "Uh, it's fine," he mumbled. "Mind showing me what you caught?" I continued. Their combined stringers accounted for 22 bass averaging from one to three pounds. And to top that off, they had a gunnysack full of big bluegills.

It was not the harvesting of so many fish that angered me that morning. The pond needed heavy harvesting. What did bother me though was that I had granted fishing permission to only the one angler; the others were uninvited. By granting permission to most of those who asked, I had put myself in a tough position for later.

So I was forced to set down stricter rules. Those with permission were informed that the right to fish was theirs only. Naturally, this offended some of them, although most continued fishing the pond after the incident. What happened though was that some of the uninvited "guests" paid no attention. Not only did many of them continue fishing the pond, but, in turn, they invited others. Hence, what was originally a snowball action turned into an avalanche of fishing pressure. Originally I had extended fishing rights as a courtesy. Now, there were some who thought of me as mean, cranky pond owner, unwilling to share the pond's bounty.

As the unwanted fishing pressure increased, so did acts of poaching and vandalism. One FISHING BY PERMISSION

ONLY sign was ripped from a post. A gate latch was torn off. And scatterings of litter became more prominent.

It was not until I requested the help of the landowner that the problem was reduced significantly. After several attempts at posting, locking the gate and limiting fishermen, I finally employed the farmer to act as caretaker. Since many of his chores were in the vicinity of the pond, he could watch it and the access road which ran in front of his house. I had introduced him to all those who had permission and he could identify them usually by color and make of car. With these measures, the number of uninvited anglers was finally curbed without too much bother. And by shaving down the number of unwanted guests, it was possible to grant permission to other anglers who stopped and asked permission. Those who observed the rules were treated to excellent bass and bluegill fishing.

Summing it up, people management was my major problem. It was a tough one to handle as are most problems arising with persons who do not respect another's property. It should be prevented by setting stiff rules right from the start.

ON THE GOOD SIDE

Problems involving weeds, water quality, rough fish or dam leakage have posed little of concern. The pond was designed deep enough to prevent heavy weed growth. Rough fish never obtained a foothold in the water, and the pond has remained healthy; it still is today. The dam has never leaked. The trickle tube and drainpipe have worked well. I credit the success of my fish pond experience to strictly following the advice of the SCS and game and fish department. No shortcuts were taken to save time or money. An enduring investment, such as a pond, is still relatively inexpensive compared to the years of enjoyment derived from it. And probably, one of the best reasons this pond has survived the years without a second stocking is sufficient harvesting. A lot of bluegills and a good number of bass are taken from it.

The glitter of newness has worn off the pond. But fish there

(SCS)

Some pond owners form clubs to share pond management knowledge.
Their experience is important to prospective pond owners.

are as fat and sassy as ever. It is mostly a matter of following a few rules. Fish ponds make unusual Christmas presents for the entire family. Also, a pond just may be the best project a group of anglers or a sportsmen's club can initiate!

14 | *Pertinent Laws and Liability*

THE POND OWNER SHOULD BE FAMILIAR WITH THE LAWS THAT affect his pond. Chances are the SCS technician and local fisheries manager will advise the new pond owner or the prospective one on current state and local water laws.

Water laws are designed primarily to protect public waters against contamination, pollution and indiscriminate stocking. They are enforced to protect public and private water rights.

Laws and regulations greatly vary from one state to another. To describe the water laws of each would take a voluminous book in itself. Rather than go into such detail, the highlights of water laws of interest to most prospective pond owners will be discussed in this chapter. They will be treated under three classifications: laws regarding Water, Fishing, and The Pond.

WATER LAWS

The key to water laws lies in the term *Water Quality*. Federal and state governments are now taking water quality guidelines seriously. Within the past decade, individuals and agencies have seen the need for protecting available water resources. Stricter water quality laws have been passed. Some states have cleaned polluted streams and rivers. Others have passed regulations which, if obeyed and enforced, will prevent pollution in waterways and insure a high quality of water. Industrial and agricultural wastes, significant causes of toxic and thermal pollution, are being treated before being discharged.

In regards to the private fish pond owner, state and federal water quality laws can affect fish ponds. Water quality has a direct bearing on the fish contained in the pond and neighboring streams and water sources. As an example, many ponds use streams for water sources. In most cases a portion of the stream is channeled into the pond. Overflow from the pond usually flows or is redirected back into the stream below the dam or spillway. If the quality of water coming from the pond is poor, it could affect both private and public portions of that stream.

Runoff from the pond, in times of heavy rainfall, could drain into other water sources, both private and public, further affecting state waters. This is the reason why some state laws include fish ponds under water quality regulations. And this is why there are such strict rules regarding the use of herbicides and algaecides in fish pond management.

Even if the fish pond does not use a stream as a water source and there is little chance of runoff affecting public waters, some states include *all waters* used for drinking, recreation, or navigation under their water quality guidelines.

States also have *Water Storage Regulations*. All impounded waters fall under these rules. For the most part these regulations are concerned with the apparatus used in controlling the impoundment's water supply. For instance, in the case of trickle tubes, some states require certain design, materials and diameter in order for the pond to qualify as having effective water controls.

Drainpipes also fall under water storage regulations. Certain states require pond owners to have them installed. They further specify that the pipe should be designed and placed in the pond in such a manner that it can be completely emptied within a specified period of time.

These regulations are designed as preventive safety measures. A well constructed, well designed trickle tube, for instance, can prevent a dam from breaking under heavy periods of rain. An adequate drainpipe permits a pond to be drained quickly in case of drowning, pollution, unknown fish mortality and dam repair.

Although some rules seem quite restrictive, most SCS designed ponds conform to standards right from the start. And during the life of a well-managed pond, chances are the owner will not feel overburdened by the necessary regulations.

There are instances when Board of Health guidelines apply to pond management. For instance, if the location of a fish pond presented a contamination hazard to the local water supply, reservoirs, springs and wells, common sources of water could be affected. A new location would be necessary. But these cases are rare. An SCS technician in his pond planning would ordinarily prevent such a situation from arising in the first place.

Suppose the pond owner allows swimming in his impoundment; the *Board of Health* could intervene under the regulations pertaining to swimming or bathing in waters unfit or polluted for such activities. But again, a well managed fish pond would neither be polluted nor unfit for swimming, so no special problems should arise here.

Water laws also fall under the category of *Water Rights*. Most of us have seen Western movies built on the theme of individuals or families involved in water rights disputes. Ordinarily, the trouble would take place when an upstream rancher or farmer impounded, channeled or in some way cut off the water supply of the landowner downstream. Without water for livestock, crops or personal consumption, of course, the downstream landowner would be forced to protect his interests or move out.

Other forms of movie plot bickering have involved powerful landowners prohibiting lessor landowners from using the water on their property. The fight for water control rights, in real life as well as in movies and the single most important ingredient in the sustenance of life, has led to modern-day water laws.

For the most part, violence in pursuit and preservation of water rights is a thing of the past. Even with fair regulations, however, some disagreement continues. Water is just too valuable a resource to "throw up for grabs."

The pond owner should be aware of the importance of water as it affects the livelihood of ranchers and farmers in his area. As a landowner, a person inherits a keen awareness of the water rights issue. But urban and suburban pond owners, those not living near the pond site but merely owners of the pond, should know how *vital* water rights are.

SCS technicians are especially concerned with water sharing. Again, as in most other phases of pond planning and management, they will guide the prospective pond owner to locations where water rights can be shared with other users.

As mentioned earlier, a secondary flow or channel of stream water is often used as a water source and diverted into the pond. If the water source is constant and reliable, there ordinarily is no problem in sharing water. Most of the flow is directed around the pond and overflow from the pond returns to the stream. Hence the landowner downstream is not deprived of water.

Some ponds are built expressly for water storage, although they usually do not make the best fish ponds. A stream that may ordinarily go dry in late summer or fall, can be kept flowing during drought periods, due to the water storage capacity of such a pond. Such an impoundment is a conservation measure that equalizes the flow over wet and dry seasons.

Crappie is one species of fish that can adapt to ponds with fluctuating water levels. Changing water levels help control crappie populations.

Nature often provides the best examples of effective water control. The beaver, for instance, is a pond builder. Water is impounded by a string of beaver ponds. I have observed small streams, devoid of beaver activity, run dry in the fall in the Rocky Mountain area while similar-size streams, marked with beaver dams and ponds, maintain a relatively constant flow throughout the year. The beaver is a good water conservationist.

Where there is an inconsistent flow of stream water, pond building is discouraged in agricultural areas. A farmer or rancher, whose livelihood may depend on that water, has priority over persons planning to use the water for recreation purposes. The farmer, in turn, may desire to build a pond to store an irregular flow. He may even derive some sport fishing from it. But the main purpose of such storage is for irrigation and water for livestock.

It goes without saying that channelization or impoundment of water from irrigation ditches, unless done by the landowner, himself, would probably violate water rights. And rarely do such water sources insure the quality water needed by most gamefish like bass, bluegill, and trout.

Before pond construction, the owner should acquaint himself with the water rights pertaining to his source of water. This is normal procedure. The pond owner should insure these rights are protected in writing and have such documents notorized. Water rights, incidentally, are as much subject to change as property rights and changes in ownership.

In the case where a stream source is regarded as public water on public land, a use arrangement with the state through the SCS technician is advised. In some instances, diversion of water may not be allowed, especially if the stretch of stream has been designated for public fishing use.

In some states all water, whether navigable or not, is the property of that state and only the access to various stretches of water can be controlled by landowners. Therefore it is the state, through the office of a water control board or game and fish agency, that has the final say-so on how the water can be used.

For a pond owner searching for a suitable pond site, this means that he may have to deal with a private landowner for access to a water source and then negotiate with state agencies for rights to that water.

To further complicate water rights issues, in some states, the landowner owns the land *under* the water; in other words, the stream bed is private property. And in other areas, the state may own the stream bed, banks and shorelines along such streams. You should be aware of these variances in water rights. Knowledgeable SCS and game and fish department personnel will offer the best advice on meeting your water needs.

Water channelization laws stem from regulations regarding water rights. Basically these laws prevent the unnecessary and indiscriminate channelization of streams and rivers. Any diversion or redirecting a stream flow or a portion of that flow is considered channelization. In most states a permit is required for channelization. The permit is usually granted where there would be no harm to existing waterways or their fish. A permit is also considered when the effects of such channelization are mutually beneficial to man, water and soil resources. Since the ecological and conservation attributes of fish ponds have already been explained, it is easy to understand why pond planners, under the auspices of SCS, are usually granted permits for channelization.

One important consideration when diverting or channeling a portion of a stream is erosion control. The ditch or channel diverting the water should be sodded. It can also be held firm with shrubs and trees. Channelization can add esthetic value, but the disastrous results of some large-scale channelization methods are quite familiar. Taking a once-meandering stream and converting it to a straight-line ditch is neither pleasing to the eye nor conducive to good fishing. A meandering channel off the main stream, especially if it covers 20 yards or more of watershed before entering into the pond, fits nature better.

FISHING LAWS

Rules pertaining to size of fish, limits, seasons and fishing methods are important to the pond owner.

An old friend of mine, the same elderly gentleman who belonged to an exclusive fishing club on the outskirts of Laramie, had quite an educational experience at his "private lake." After investing a goodly portion of cash into the fishing rights, Andy assumed that he did not need a state fishing license. But in February he learned different. Ordinarily he would have purchased a Wyoming resident fishing license, for his license from the year before had expired. But he figured his membership dues made the purchase of a new license unnecessary.

A thick ice lid covered the lake when Andy arrived. Eight-inch catchable trout had been planted in the pond the previous fall. He wanted to get a jump on the fishing. After boring several holes and trying five or six different locations, he found some hot spots where he caught rainbows weighing from one to two pounds—small-headed, deep-chested specimens. His fast action was soon interrupted, however. A local warden stopped at the lake and walked out to check Andy's success. "Fishing's great," my friend volunteered. "Good," answered the warden, "Mind if I see your license?" "License? I don't need a license here. I paid good money to catch these fish. They aren't stocked by the game and fish department." "You still need a state license to fish here," the warden retorted. Andy was whipped; he ended up paying a $16 fine, plus having to relinquish his stringer of fish.

Most state game and fish departments require that anglers have in possession a current and valid fishing license when fishing *any* of the state, just as they require hunters to carry hunting licenses even when hunting private land.

Also in effect are state rules and regulations regarding size and weight limits of fish. Specified seasons for sport fishing also apply to private fish ponds—in some states. In addition, there are regulations that specify the type of fishing equipment that can be used. And certain types of baits or angling methods are prohibited.

After working with SCS technicians and state fisheries biologists, it is doubtful that the average pond owner will be negligent about fishing regulations. The only cases I discovered were where pond owners had assumed that the fishing rules were not *enforced* at their pond. But very few pond owners deliberately break fish and game laws.

Some states, nevertheless, give the private pond owner more leeway than others. Private hunting or shooting preserves, for example, are governed by their own set of seasons, limits and licenses. U-Ketchum fishing ponds, too, may be regulated by different sets of rules.

Some states do not enforce seasons on private fish ponds. This helps the owner maintain a desired harvest. Size, number and weight limits are also more liberal.

The most universal game and fish requirement among states is that state fishing licenses are required when fishing. Some states also require pond owners to have a private fish pond permit in addition to the fishing licenses.

There are reasons for imposing state game and fish laws on private ponds. Aside from measures of control, ponds stocked by state or federal agencies may properly be subject to state regulations. Such rules often discourage poaching and trespassing on private fish ponds. And there are benefits to the state in the extra revenue from the license sales; it is used for the state's fishery program. Since state and federal assistance may be offered to the pond owner, it is reasonable to expect enforcement of state fishing regulations.

Public access has been mentioned briefly. Some states offer assistance in stocking programs for private pond owners. In turn, some of these states require these pond owners to open their ponds to public fishing. There are states, of course, that lend stocking assistance but do not require public access. Just as the Bureau of Sport Fisheries does *not* require a pond owner to allow public fishing if it assists in stocking new ponds.

To prevent misunderstanding in regards to public access, seek advice of public stocking agencies before stocking plans are made. A pond owner may find that state stocking programs help cut expenses of fish pond operations. By allowing limited public access, a desired fish harvest can be obtained. On the other hand, unlimited public fishing may offer numerous people management problems for the pond owner. In this case, it would possibly be cheaper to restock fingerlings purchased from private hatcheries.

When considering public access in cases where individuals or sportsmen's groups are purchasing the immediate pond area, the landowner should be considered first. Public access to the pond, even if expected in just a limited number, may cause the landowner problems. The future of the fish pond could thus be jeopardized. Firm commitments regarding public access must be thoroughly discussed and decided upon by the landowner, pond owner and SCS representative.

There are several states with *Stocking Laws*. Few problems result when the pond owner follows advice from SCS and game and fish departments on what species to stock. But an ill-informed pond owner can unknowingly violate stocking laws prohibiting the introduction of certain fish species to waters within the state. These laws, after all, are provided to protect established fish populations; desirable fish species, suitable to the area, could be damaged by careless stocking measures.

Most states require permits for seining (private waters included), fee fishing, commercial fish farming, bait minnow raising and sale of bait minnows. Except for seining, these permits are aimed at regulating commercial operations. Seining permits are designed to control the species of bait minnows used in public and private waters. For example, minnows seined from one stream and used or sold as bait for another stream, could harm existing fisheries. Using a system requiring seining permits insures that only specified kinds of minnows may be seined and sold as bait.

Seining is also a poacher's tool. Under certain conditions, it is a method by which a fish stealer can harvest illegally a large quantity of fish in but a short period of time. Although poachers have slight regard for the law, registered seiners in an area are usually known and recognized by the authorities. They then are free to concentrate on weeding out those seining illegally.

LAWS REGARDING THE POND ITSELF

In the chapter on pond construction, building plans, water control devices and approved construction materials were discussed. There is no need to dwell further on the methods and materials used in pond construction except to say that some states have laws regarding them. For example, several states require that pond plans be approved by registered, professional engineers before construction proceeds. Other states stipulate that pond design must comply with state laws regarding structure, and permits must be secured before construction takes place. SCS technicians are familiar with such planning and construction permits and advise pond owners in such matters.

In treating ponds or fish, a permit is needed for the use of herbicides, algaecides or piscicides. Upon the recommendations and advice of qualified technicians for such treatments the permits are obtainable through the SCS, game and fish department or Board of Health.

Certain states also regulate the use of mineral and organic fertilizers. Since there is the possibility of fertilization applications affecting public water and land, some states retain control over pond fertilization.

Pond drainage laws have been discussed under state water storage regulations. States can require drainpipes capable of draining the pond within a stipulated period of time.

There always seem to be questions on *Pond Liability Laws*, particularly as to a pond owner's liability. When a pond owner lets a friend or a segment of the public fish the pond, what liabilities does he incur? More specifically, in case of accidental drowning is there any way the pond owner is liable? Or, in case of an accident in the water or around the pond area, to what extent, if any, is the owner liable?

Unfortunately, there are few concrete decisions concerning pond owner liability which apply to any and all cases. But the pond owner is ordinarily not liable in accidental drownings and as to injuries in and around the pond.

The more anglers that fish a pond, the greater the chance of accidents. The accident risk increases when boats are used for fishing. The pond owner who rents or lends his boat to others is walking a thin line over the liability issue, especially if the boat or motor is faulty or defective in some way. A claim could be made that a defective boat or motor caused a death or injury.

In regards to swimming, risks are certainly being taken. But chances of the pond owner being liable are slim.

Limiting the area and the number of persons using the pond is probably the best way to minimize liability risk. There are other ways to be on the safe side, too.

Riding stable owners, float trip operators and tour guides—

persons who operate recreational services where some risk of accidents is involved—ordinarily take precautions. Most often, their customers sign release forms which state flatly "RIDE, FLOAT OR HIKE AT YOUR OWN RISK. We are in no way responsible for injuries or death suffered from accidents." Many concessions display large signs emphasizing their disclaimer of liability.

Disclaiming liability is not unique with outdoor recreation concessionaires. By examining the fine print on tickets to various athletic events, one can read similar disclaimers. They are common in baseball, especially where there is always the possibility of a spectator being hit by a baseball. But major league clubs and stadium owners warn spectators on the back of tickets that they will not be responsible for any accidents or injuries.

For the pond owner, use of signed liability waiver forms may be necessary if limited or complete public access is allowed. Otherwise posted signs saying FISH OR SWIM AT YOUR OWN RISK may be adequate. But if he has been

(SCS)

A boat is fun and good for fishing a pond, but the pond owner should be aware of liability laws which cover the use of his boat by others.

duly warned, perhaps even if he has signed a waiver of liability, someone still might sue you—and worse yet, collect! If a small bridge, for instance, is put across one neck of the pond, the owner is responsible for its proper upkeep, repair and reasonable hazard-free condition. In this respect, the pond owner is much in the same liability position as the average homeowner.

Available to the pond owner, however, is specialty insurance which covers pond liability. Its cost varies from company to company. Since low risk is usually involved, the rates are not ordinarily high. Swimming pool owners often take out such policies to protect themselves if friends or neighbors are allowed to swim. So before the pond is filled, it would be wise to check with insurance agents on a policy designed for your needs.

15 | *Fun with Fish*

IN ANOTHER CHAPTER I RECALLED SOME OF MY FONDEST EXPERIENCES with fish ponds. They happened "just being with the pond." Observation, studying water ecology, underwater observation— these are ways to have fun with fish. Raising fish from fingerlings to maturity is an interesting hobby in itself. The fish pond, a larger scale version of the glass aquarium, presents quite a showcase of aquatic life.

It is important to remember that adequate fish harvest is essential to the well being of the fish population. Despite the fun of just observing and studying fish, harvest plays a vital role. Without it, overpopulation would surely result. Then would follow the stunting and die-offs which could cancel out any long-term enjoyable relationship between the fish, the pond and its owner.

OBSERVING AND LEARNING ABOUT FISH

A dock may serve as both a useful observation and fishing spot. The structure makes it possible to observe fish in the deeper water. Deeper water is usually clearer.

Trout

Trout are usually found in schools, especially when the fish are all approximately the same size. The very large and the smaller fish tend to forage by themselves. Under pond conditions, trout rarely are stationary. They move around the pond, and at different depths. For the most part, they are searching for food, both aquatic underwater and terrestial morsels that may have blown on the surface. In a stream, trout will be scattered, taking favored feeding positions according to their size and weight, facing upstream. They face the current in order to be in position to devour drifting food. They are also this way better able to maintain their stability, just as a plane takes off and lands into the wind. In most ponds, however, the current is negligible, therefore the trout tend to bunch up and move together in search of food.

In early morning and late afternoon, trout frequent the shallow parts of the pond. This is primarily for feeding and it is the best time of day to observe them. The sun's angle allows the observer to see into the water. In the midday there's usually too much glare for good viewing. The calmest days, naturally, are the best days for observation. Polaroid sunglasses help cut glare on the water and are very useful.

Although *rainbow trout* do not spawn successfully in most ponds, the spawning urge is present in the spring with the month dependent upon water temperature. May and June are usually considered prime spawning seasons in trout states. Rainbows then invade the shallows where they will mill around in three to five feet of water without any apparent rhyme or reason for their behavior.

Some pond owners are fortunate enough to have conditions suitable for spawning. A shallow, gravel-bottomed source of stream water usually fits the bill. At times the water will barely cover the backs of spawning trout, when egg laying, fertilization and hatching processes take place. For the observer, the natural spawning processes are interesting. Intruder fish are forced away from the spawning area. Males guard eggs with the ferocity of a sow bear protecting cubs. Predator fish, those natural to such a spawning stream, attempt to eat some of the eggs. The process is a life and death struggle designed by nature to insure the procreation of the species.

More often than during spawning, trout pond owners watch rainbows dimpling the surface for insects during the evening "rise." Trout have various ways of feeding according to season and type of food. Mosquitoes and gnats, for instance, cause trout to explode from the water. Sometimes they seem suspended above the water when leaping for mosquitoes. This is surface feeding frenzy.

Other times, saucer-sized swirls are evident on the pond's surface. But the water is not as violently disturbed as in surface feeding activities. Chances are the trout are rising and swirling for aquatic insects as they ascend from the pond's bottom to the surface. Trout grab the insects before they can reach the surface. Many varieties of insect larva hatch by this process. They form wings and fly beyond the grasp of trout within seconds after hitting the surface.

At times trout are stationed near the surface waiting for hatching insects. Only the swirls of their tails are evident as they lunge for food. Other times they may be stationed a bit deeper and cannot be seen. The only hint of feeding then is a mighty swirl of water, often accompanied by a sucking or gurgling noise.

Fly fishermen are sometimes fooled when trout feed in this manner. On occasion a trout may attack a rising larva and miss it. Not giving up easily, they will often make a second swipe at the morsel of food while it is on the surface. The water explodes. Anglers diagnose the hatch as surface terrestrials. They choose dry flies for the feeding fish and are usually skunked. A trout feeding on rising aquatics is very selective. Success in matching the hatch comes when the rising action of the real insect is matched, a technique mastered by few anglers. The size and color of the fly must be perfect.

There are times when trout stick almost exclusively to bottom feeding. Aquatic insects, before the hatching stage, constitute most of their diet. Observing them at this time, ordinarily during cold or cool temperatures, is impossible unless the water is exceptionally clear.

The cloudiness of fertile water often hampers observation. But it is better to have a fertile pond than to sacrifice fish growth and weed control measures in favor of fish watching. Periods in the fall and spring, before fertilization, are good times for observation. Quality trout water should be clear then, just as it is several weeks after fertilization has taken place.

Brook trout lend themselves to different methods of observation. Spawning requirements are similar to rainbow trout with the exception that brookies spawn in the fall of the year—usually in September or October, depending on water temperatures.

If there is no suitable spawning stream available, look for them in the shallows. Going through spawning rituals, brook trout will mill in numbers similar to the rainbow.

Brookies display acrobatic feeding performances just as eagerly as rainbows early in the morning and evening. They are especially active surface feeders during periods of little or no wind. They approach surface insects quicker and with more force than rainbow trout. Where the rainbow will often appear to inhale a mosquito or grasshopper on the water, a brook trout attacks it with head-shaking, tail-slapping authority. Brook trout display erratic swimming motions in their approach to food; whereas the rainbows' reactions seem slower and more deliberate. In a pond containing both species, you will soon learn to detect brook trout from rainbows by their feeding tactics. As an angler, this will help in selecting the right fly or lure.

Bluegill

Most of the same fish observation techniques apply to warm water species. I find bass and bluegill more cooperative than trout. Bluegills, especially, are fun to watch on their spawning

Observing fish feeding habits is part of the fish raising fun.

nests in spring or early summer. The beds, often gravel, sand or mud depressions cleared of weeds in a near circular fashion, are built in shallow water. Watching the female guard the nest is something! She is an aggressive guardian. I have observed six-inch bluegills chasing 15-inch bass and large snapping turtles from the nest area. Frantically charging, retreating and swiping with their tails, bluegills outbluff many larger fish in the pond environment.

Such aggressiveness over spawning beds makes bluegills relatively easy to catch in spring and summer. They attack a worm or fly with the same ferociousness as they scare off intruders. I have led a six-inch floating minnow lure through a bluegill spawning ground only to have it attacked by swarms of bluegills not yet quite as long as the lure, itself. One time while fishing for bass, I hooked a five-inch bluegill on a six-inch plug.

If not bothered, rarely will bluegill leave the nest. Many times these fish will be still for long periods at a time—only a slight fanning of tail anl fins keeping them in position. Other times, they skirt the outer rim of the nest at a methodical pace. And at times of obvious alarm, sunfish speed frantically around the nest for as long as a minute.

In feeding exhibitions, bluegills occasionally rise to the surface for food. However, my observations have shown that young, smaller fish are more active at surface feeding than the larger bluegills that feed mainly below the surface.

To the fisherman, the small bluegill often presents a problem. They beat the larger bluegills, feeding deeper, to the bait. This is why in fish pond management, it is often necessary to remove large numbers of small bluegills. Their tendency towards overpopulation makes them a challenge to manage.

Large bluegills move for food in swift, straight lines of attack. Since their mouths are especially small, they ordinarily cannot fit whole worms or grasshoppers into them. So they hit the worms or insects hard—often tearing off a piece. They return quickly to follow up their meal. Smaller fish stand by in hopes of picking up leftover morsels. At times, when small fish move in to help with the eating, a large fish will run them off. In the meantime, other smaller fish move in for the remainder of the meal.

Bluegills probably are such aggressive fighters because of their fierce competition for food. When a bluegill is hungry, there is no half-hearted attack on bait.

Bluegills are found in the shallows early and late in the day. During midday they frequent greater depths and position themselves in favored holes. During this time, they can be tempermental feeders. And the observer looking for sunfish at midday may falsely believe all bluegill life has vanished.

Bass

Bass, even the young ones, are more deliberate in every manner when compared to the sunfish. As young fish, they often travel in large schools. But some five-inchers break from the schools. Frequenting the shallows early and late, single fish appear perfectly still in the water. I have often looked in shallow, clear water for some time before spotting a "log" bass.

As bass grow larger, they are still found in schools, but there always seems to be a certain number that are loners. In a pond with a good bass population, several individual bass can be seen cruising the shallows for food early in the morning.

They look for small sunfish or minnows. Artificial baits, re-sembling their breakfast food, almost certainly produce quick action.

Even as youngsters, the large mouth of the species is evi-dent. I have watched six-inch bass attack and swallow sunfish of four inches. I have deep-hooked ten-inch bass on six-inch floating minnow plugs. When attacking baits, they come full blast with mouths open wide.

Mature bass are interesting feeders. They are savagely ag-gressive. It seems to me that many of the fish caught have ended up on stringers because of their sheer meanness.

I have watched two-pound bass laying in the shallows, still as logs and very much resembling them. A school of bait fish will swarm like bees into the bass' lair. Still the bass remains motionless. The fish permits the minnows to come within range—a foot or so away. Then in a lightning quick movement, the largemouth shoots into the midst of the bait-fish, devouring several and crippling others. In shallow water this action resembles a torpedo hitting its target. Minnows often skip and jump above the surface—some from the force of the strike, others in a frantic effort to escape.

Because of the bass' aggressiveness, the fish is fun to ob-serve. His unpredictable nature often leads to the unexpected. One evening I was planting some oak trees near the pond when my eye caught the trail of a small frog swimming across the water. The frog had about 30 feet to swim before reaching the opposite shore. But then another wake erupted from the shallows. The two creatures were on a collision course when I saw the head and open mouth of a bass above the water's sur-face. When the two met, the frog never had a chance. The bass disappeared with a tail-slapping dive.

On another occasion I saw a two-foot water snake inhaled by a three-pound bass. Only the snake's head and top part of his body was visible. A swirl of water from the nearest bank signaled that a bass was interested in a snake dinner. The fish followed its victim for ten yards before the bass dived and exploded the surface with the snake dangling from its jaws.

Observing bass in spring and early summer is possible because then the fish are in shallow water spawning. Fiercely protective in spawning, they attack anything that enters the area. In states where specified fishing seasons for bass have been set, fishing is usually delayed until after prime spawning times.

A dock is especially useful in observing warm water species. Both bass and bluegill favor the shade of docks and often congregate there. Some of the best fishing I've experienced has been near docks.

Other ways to observe fish include netting or seining them for closer inspection, but an important thing to remember is that frequent fish handling may lead to disease and parasites. If the mucus that encases a fish is rubbed off, or the fish is injured in handling, that fish is susceptible to disease. Treat fish gently and shake them from the net without handling them.

Fish traps, similar to smaller, commercially sold minnow traps, catch fish. And the fish can be released without handling them. By trapping fish, you can learn varying degrees of fish intelligence. For example, small bass, bluegill and trout are relatively easy to trap. But as the fish mature, they become wary and will ordinarily not fall for trapping techniques.

ECOLOGY

Fish ecology, that is the study of fish in relation to its environment, was referred to briefly in an earlier chapter. The study of fish ecology is a complete science in itself. Pond owners, in one way or another, become associated with pond ecology. The degree to which they pursue this fascinating subject is a matter of personal interest. But some pond owners derive just as much satisfaction from learning about fish as they do in catching them.

If a pond owner is really serious about learning more on fish ecology, enrolling in a college course would be rewarding. Universities and some junior colleges now have such courses. In one semester, the pond owner can build a strong foundation in matters relating to the life cycles of fish and their environment. Game and fish departments also sometimes offer short courses in fish ecology. And in some areas local fisheries biologists conduct seminars on the subject.

An alternative to attending classes is reading books written on the subject. Local fisheries biologists or culturists can recommend titles to pond owners. Information on where to obtain such reading will be provided by your state's Information and Education Division of the game and fish department.

Chances are most of us want to learn as much as we can about fish ecology without really delving too deeply into the intricate science, formulas and complexities of the subject. Local fisheries experts can recommend pamphlets on fish ecology, and these experts are glad to share personal knowledge with interested pond owners.

In its basic stage, fish ecology is quite simple. You may even be unaware of the learning process made possible by your pond and its environment. Observation is the key to learning. Whether you are fishing or waiting for the fish in the pond to grow larger, awareness of the fish environment teaches many facets of fish ecology that books cannot.

(SCS)

Just plain observing and studying fish is fun.

Simple investigative projects can give you a greater understanding of this science. Projects that go hand-in-hand with good fish pond management make clear the dependence of fish upon quality water.

UNDERWATER OBSERVATION

Underwater observation can be undertaken in several ways. It can be as simple as swimming underwater with mask and snorkel. Or it can lead to SCUBA (Self-Contained Underwater Breathing Apparatus) diving. Either way, provided the pond is clear enough to see underwater, the pond owner who joins the fish in their environment is in for special treats.

Snorkeling

The simplest method of underwater observation is with mask, snorkel and fins. This gear enables a swimmer to stay underwater for some length of time. The mask enables clear vision. Fins allow an observer to cover greater water areas and the snorkel or air tube gives swimmers an uninterrupted view below the water. Although relatively inexpensive compared to SCUBA gear, good quality snorkel gear is important. Good equipment makes underwater observation more enjoyable. Quality gear can be obtained through reputable sporting goods dealers and diving equipment shops.

Scuba Diving

SCUBA diving gives an observer much the same freedom of the fish. It is the ultimate form of underwater observation. Ordinarily fish are not afraid of divers joining them at their level. Fish then can be observed from a few feet away and be photographed with underwater camera.

Mask, fins and snorkel are essential to SCUBA diving. Compressed air tanks serve as the diver's oxygen supply and enable swimmers to stay underwater for periods of 30 to 60 minutes at a time. The purchase of air tanks and regulators should be done only upon the advice of experts and at reputable dive shops that specialize in such equipment. SCUBA lessons are essential for safety and complete enjoyment of the sport.

In addition to tanks and regulators, SCUBA divers sometimes wear wet suits (to keep warm and to protect the body), floatation jackets and weight belts.

Underwater Photography

Underwater photography is possible with snorkeling and SCUBA methods. Watertight housings are available for most popular 35mm and movie cameras. And some cameras are built watertight. They can withstand pressures of 160 feet. Such cameras are small, relatively inexpensive and simple to operate. Diving equipment shops have information on them and on appropriate housings.

Photographing the fish in your pond opens a spectacular world of fun with fish. There is an element of stalking involved— getting close enough for a good photo. The excitement comes in clicking the shutter, knowing you have captured a fish in its own environment. Observation comes first-hand and the experience lasts as long as the photo in your album.

Underwater photo techniques are covered in detail in book-let form available from leading camera shops and film manu-facturers.

Sport fishing will provide you with the greatest share of fun with fish. But don't overlook the possibilities mentioned in this chapter. The underwater world you created is open to inspec-tion. The degree of enjoyment derived from that world is your choice. The better you know all facets of pond life, the greater the return from the investment.

Bibliography

PAMPHLETS

America Goes Fishing Dept of Interior-Fish & Wildlife Service, Conservation Note 14, April, 1964.

Anderson, Wallace L., and Lawrence V. Compton. *More Wildlife through Soil and Water Conservation.* USDA-SCS, Agriculture Information Bulletin No. 175.°

Assistance Available from the Soil Conservation Service. USDA Agriculture Information Bulletin No. 345, October, 1970.

Borell, Adrey E., and Paul M. Scheffer. *Trout in Farm and Ranch Ponds.* USDA, Farmers' Bulletin No. 2154, October, 1966.°

Bussey, Gene R. *Back Yard Aquaculture.* Life Support Systems, Inc. Albuquerque, New Mexico.

Central Nevada Resource Conservation and Development Project. USDA-SCS, March, 1971.

Conservation Directory 1970. National Wildlife Federation. Washington, D.C.

Dasmann, Raymond F. *An Environment Fit For People.* Public

Affairs Committee, Inc., Public Affairs Pamphlet No. 421, 1969.

Dillard, Joe G., and Max Hamilton. *Evaluation of Two Stocking Methods for Missouri Farm Ponds.* Missouri Dept of Conservation, Division of Fisheries, D-J Series, No. 7, October, 1969.

Dillon, Olan W., Jr., William W. Neely, Verne E. Davison, and Lawrence V. Compton. *Warm-water Fishponds.* USDA-SCS, Farmers' Bulletin No. 2250, December, 1971. *

Facts about Resource Conservation and Development Projects. USDA-SCS-CI-14, September, 1970.

Federal Assistance to Outdoor Recreation. Dept of Interior-Bureau of Outdoor Recreation, Publication No. 1, 1966. *

Fish Ponds: Construction and Management in Pennsylvania. Pennsylvania State University, College of Agriculture, Special Circular 78, Natural Resource Series.

Fox, Arthur J., Jr. (Ed.), *Engineering News-Record.* McGraw-Hill, Inc., Vol. 189, No. 12, September 21, 1972.

Grizzell, Roy A., Jr., Olan W. Dillon, Jr., and Edward G. Sullivan. *Catfish Farming.* USDA-SCS, Farmers' Bulletin No. 2244, November, 1969.

Heiney, Clayton L. *A Survey of Recreational Benefits and Uses of Farm Ponds in Pennsylvania.* USDA-SCS, 1967.

King, Willis. *Survey of Fishing in 1000 Ponds in 1959.* Dept of Interior-Fish Hatcheries and Fishery Management Services, Fish and Wildlife Circular 86, May, 1960.

Let's Grow. USDA-SCS, Agriculture Information Bulletin 337, 1969. *

Lopinot, A. C. *Pond Fish and Fishing in Illinois.* Illinois Dept of Conservation, Fishery Bulletin No. 5, 1968.

Marriage, L. Dean, and Verne E. Davison. *Fish Ponds—Construction and Management.* (From *A Manual of Wildlife Conservation,* Wildlife Society, 1971.)

Marriage, L. Dean, Adrey E. Borell, and Paul M. Scheffer. *Trout Ponds for Recreation.* USDA-SCS, Farmers' Bulletin No. 2249, November, 1971. *

Neely, W. W., Verne E. Davison, and Lawrence V. Compton. *Warm Water Ponds for Fishing.* USDA-SCS, Farmers' Bulletin No. 2210, May, 1965. *

Neely, William W., and Verne E. Davison. *Wild Ducks on Farmland in the South.* USDA-SCS, Farmers' Bulletin No. 2218, March, 1971. *

North Cal-Neva RC&D Project. USDA-SCS, 1968.

Parasites and Diseases of Warm-water Fishes. Dept of Interior-Bureau of Sport Fisheries & Wildlife, Bureau Resource Publication 76, May, 1969.

Pondfish Hatchery. Dept of Interior-Bureau of Sport Fisheries & Wildlife, RP-58. *

Ponds for Fishing. Missouri Dept of Conservation. 1968.

Ponds for Water Supply and Recreation. USDA-SCS, Agriculture Handbook No. 387, January, 1971.*

RC&D-The Can-do Projects. (Reprinted from *Soil Conservation.* USDA-SCS, 1969.)

Scheffer, Paul M., and L. Dean Marriage. *Trout Farming.* USDA-SCS, Leaflet 552, November, 1969.*

Sediment. USDA-SCS, Agriculture Information Bulletin No. 325.*

Six Questions Everybody Asks at National Fish Hatcheries. Dept of Interior-Bureau of Sport Fisheries & Wildlife, Circular 157.*

Trout Hatchery. Dept of Interior-Bureau of Sport Fisheries & Wildlife, RP-57.

AVAILABLE TECHNICAL NOTES AND LOCAL SPECIFICATIONS

By State and Topical Areas:

Colorado: *Fish Pond Specifications and Management, Private and Commercial*

Georgia: *Fish Pond Stocking*

Idaho: *Fish Pond Specifications, Stocking, and Management*

Kansas: *Fish Pond Specifications, Stocking, and Management*

Maine: *Fish Pond Management*

Maryland: *Fish Pond Management*

Massachusetts: *Fish Pond Management*

Michigan: *Fish Pond Specifications*

Nevada: *Fish Pond Specifications*

New Mexico: *List of Publications on Fish Culture and Related Subjects; Fish Pond Specifications and Management*

North Dakota: *Fish Pond Stocking*

Oregon: *Fish Pond Specifications, Stocking, and Management*

Pennsylvania: *Fish Pond Specifications and Management*

South Dakota: *Fish Pond Specifications and Management*

Utah: *Fish Pond Specifications, Stocking, and Management*

Vermont: *Fish Pond Specifications, Stocking, and Management*

Wyoming: *Fish Planting, Fishing Preserve, and Commerciel Hatchery Information; Fish Pond Specifications*

* For sale by the Superintendent of Documents, U.S. Government Printing Office, Washington, D.C. 20402